I0037324

The Passive Income Blueprint Credit Cards and Credit Repair:

How to Repair Your Credit Score, Increase Your Credit Score, Leverage Credit Lines and Travel for Free Using Credit Card Rewards and Points

By

Income Mastery

Table of Contents

© **Copyright 2019 by Income Mastery - All rights reserved**.

This document is geared towards providing exact and reliable information in regard to the topic and issue covered. The publication is sold with the idea that the publisher is not required to render accounting, officially permitted, or otherwise, qualified services. If advice is necessary, legal or professional, a practiced individual in the profession should be ordered.

From a Declaration of Principles which was accepted and approved equally by a Committee of the American Bar Association and a Committee of Publishers and Associations.

In no way is it legal to reproduce, duplicate, or transmit any part of this document in either electronic means or in printed format. Recording of this publication is strictly prohibited and any storage of this document is not allowed unless with written permission from the publisher. All rights reserved.

The information provided herein is stated to be truthful and consistent, in that any liability, in terms of inattention or otherwise, by any usage or abuse of any policies, processes, or directions contained within is the solitary and utter responsibility of the recipient reader. Under no circumstances will any legal responsibility or blame be held against the publisher for any reparation, damages, or monetary loss due to the information herein, either directly or indirectly.

Respective authors own all copyrights not held by the publisher.

The information herein is offered for informational purposes solely, and is universal as so. The presentation of the information is without contract or any type of guarantee assurance.

The trademarks that are used are without any consent, and the publication of the trademark is without permission or backing by the trademark owner. All trademarks and brands within this book are for clarifying purposes only and are the owned by the owners themselves, not affiliated with this document.

Introduction

If you have picked up this book, you have likely done so because you are interested in learning more about credit cards, credit scores, and credit history. Maybe you are someone who is hoping to improve their own credit score. Maybe you are hoping to fix dings on your credit report? Maybe you simply want to know what you should be doing with your good credit or how all of this can play into owning a business. Whatever the case, this book promises to educate you on matters related to credit scores, credit cards, credit history, and funding for businesses.

By the end of the book you can expect to know what influences your credit score, how to get your credit score to go higher, how to leverage credit cards for your own gain, and how your credit cards can be used as one option to fund a new business venture. The chapters build on each other and review earlier discussed information, so you learn as you go and don't forget everything very easily.

If you're ready to change your current financial state for the better, than what are you waiting for? Jump to chapter one, and let's begin this journey.

What is Consumer Credit?

In this chapter, I'm going to guide you through the history of consumer credit and introduce all the different ways we use it today. Many people consider these financial systems to be birthed from a modern nation, but in actuality, systems such as these have been around for almost as long as humans have existed. It's important to familiarize yourself with these concepts as you work towards improving your credit score, fixing dings on your credit history, and learning how to use credit cards to your advantage. By knowing the history and important points of consumer credit, you can then use the knowledge to grow your credit, maximize your benefits, and improve your credit history.

Consumer Credit Through the Ages: A brief history

The history of consumer credit dates back to the age of antiquity, going back as far as 3,500 BC. The ancient civilizations of Sumer, Babylon, and ancient Rome (among many others) used lines of credit and loans as a means to lend land for agriculture. They also often charged a type of interest on loans. In this era and beyond, people also did not want to deal with the burden of carrying around gold or loaded bags of coins. So people started to pay for items via "credit". Fast forward to the year 800 and beyond, and people start to become concerned with the moral aspect of lending. The church became involved in financial matters by declaring that heavy interests were more damaging than beneficial, and not virtuous. Given that this was when the church led the people, people obeyed. People stopped loaning out money, land, and goods. There was less of a reason to do so if they were not going to make a lot of by charging interest. Since a variety of opportunities were no longer being funded after the lack of loans (new businesses for example) many of the civilizations stopped growing as quickly as they had been.

The modern funding of credit lines, credit scores, and reporting, however, began in England in the early 1800's. In the first few years of the 1800's, there were a group of tailors who came together to discuss which clients were failing to pay their debts and where. This hush-hush, word of mouth version of credit reporting continued through the next century with various craftsmen going so far as to write newsletters calling out which customers had failed to pay their debt. The embarrassment of being called out often prompted people to pay, or it advised certain business not to lend to the same borrowers. It was not until the year 1899 however, that an official credit score company began. The Retail Credit Company began gathering information to create a ledger of "credit-worthy" customers for companies to access. They changed their name some odd years later to Equifax. This company is the oldest credit company to exist. This was the first "official" business to create a compilation of credit history and credibility.

It wasn't until the 1930's however that credit lines actually boomed. Around that time people were able to purchase affordable appliances on lines of credit granted by department stores. Consumerism was making waves as people sought out other ways to distract themselves from the fear of war. This led to many American's having multiple lines of credit in order to afford their growing desires for material goods. Then the Diner's Club joined in creating an easier way for people to manage their credit lines. The Diner's Club created accounts that allowed for borrowers to use their accounts at multiple places while only paying one monthly payment. This was one of the first forms of the modern "credit card". Only a few years later all major banks began offering lines of credit on credit cards that could be used in most restaurants. Now, credit scores and lines of credit are part of our everyday life.

They influence the things we have access to buying, renting, and owning. Credit is equally as important not only in how we spend our money, but what we have access.

The Need for a Credit Rating System

The original form of credit ratings was a word of mouth system that involved people keeping each other informed about who was making payments towards their debt and who was not. But this was not the most useful or wise way to go about keeping track of who could make payments. People make mistakes, people act vengeful and lie, but outside of that, this also did not work for informing non-locals about a person who could not make their payments. Thus, The Retail Company stepped in to help solve this issue.

As we mentioned, lines of credit were being given out like candy by the time we got to the 1930's, prior to that period people were granted lines of credit for big purchases like cars but not for general day to day expenses. The Retail Company originally housed all related information on index cards in a complex filing system in an office. Their employees would avidly read news reports, marriage reports, arrest reports, and any other information they could find to try to find out which customers had been arrested, married, or faced some other issue that may make them less likely to pay their bills on time.

The Retail Company developed a numerical system to give to companies who wanted to know how likely a customer was to make their payments and to do so in a timely manner. The method they used then, of a rating system from 350 to 800 is the basic system that is still used today. The reports included information about their payment history, how much they owed and to who, how long they had credit at the time of application, the credit types they used, and any other recent applications. The Retail Company, now known as Equifax, clearly developed a great system because much of what was originally designed remains the same.

Now, this amount of information had the potential to greatly damage or benefit a person's life, which is why in 1970, people saw the case of "The Fair Credit Act" which changed credit reporting for the better in many ways. It stated that credit reporting companies had to follow certain limitations when accessing credit history, and when sharing those details with others. It also stated how long a credit issue could remain on file for a person. It also limited who could see this information. Before this, anyone could access information about someone's credit, which was damaging in terms of employment and relationships for some people. There has to be an initiated relationship between a creditor and the consumer for them to access their credit records. It can also be used for insurance and mortgage purposes.

Types of Consumer Credit

It is important to understand the various types of consumer credit as it will give you key insight into your credit score, and how certain purchases affect your credit score. Without this information, you might feel more inclined to take on a certain debt without realizing that it has the power to also affect you. There are three types of consumer credits that are used for various purchases. Non-installment credit, installment closed-end credit, and revolving open-end credit. Here are their key features:

1.   Non-installment Credit: This line of credit is seen most often in department stores. It is a short-term line of credit that involves one down payment, with the remainder of the debt being paid off within a short time frame (typically 1-3 months). It is typically paid off in only one, or a few, payments before the end of the loaning

timeline. This allows the consumer to take home the item they are purchasing before paying it off. This creates future sales for the department store as they know they have more income coming in from these small lines of credit, without having to lend out a large sum of money or goods.

2.   Installment Closed-End Credit: This line of credit, like the prior one, also deals with a set amount or total. This is used often for larger purchases, where the entire sum is split into payments with interest and the consumer can take the product home immediately. The payments usually span a year or more. Car loans typically fall under this category, as do department store sales for larger items (furniture or large appliances). The lender gives the item to the consumer but does not allow them to purchase more items with more credit until the original debt is paid off. The payments must be completed within the timeline assigned. Also, the creditor retains official ownership of the item until it is paid in full. If a consumer fails to make payments, the creditor has the option to take back the item and resell it to fulfill the rest of the debt. This is why we see car repossessions, and why you avoid defaulting on these type of loans at all costs.

3.   Revolving Open-End Credit: This is the kind of credit that is dealt out by most credit card companies. It is usually in the thousand-dollar range ($1,000 or as much as $10,000). Here, the creditor gives a line of credit to the consumer with a set amount that is calculated using the details from the consumer's credit report. The creditor gives the consumer the line of credit and the consumer has the freedom to decide how much of it they use and when they pay it back in full. The consumer must make payments (often they are monthly) but they can decide whether to make the minimum or pay more than the minimum amount in the payment. There is usually an associated interest fee, but the credit rating also determines how much this fee is, and when it begins on the purchases.

- There are some open lines of credit that require the consumer to pay it off in full within a certain time , such as some American Express lines of credit, but typically there is a lot of freedom and responsibility within these lines of credit. It is up to the individual to decide just how much they use from the line of credit, when they pay it off, and whether to keep the account open or not.

Now that you know the main types of credit line you can begin to learn more about how they affect your score, how you can improve your score, and how to leverage their benefits.

Understanding Your Credit Report

What is a credit report, exactly?

A credit report is given by a credit bureau and includes a rating of the consumer's overall credit history. The report includes a detailed credit history such as information regarding payment habits, open lines of credit, and financial information. This information is then given to the person requesting the report and allows them to decide the loan-worthiness of an individual. Creditors also use this information to decide how much of an interest rate to offer, the length of payments, in addition to deciding whether to loan you credit or not.

The information on your credit score comes from your creditors. They are not required to give details about everything, but most companies report to at least one credit reporting bureau. Here are some other details that will be found on your credit report:

- Your full name and any other associated names you have used in the past.
- Place of residence both current and past.

- Important information like your birth date and social security number.
- Contact information.
- Your current lines of credit along with what kind of credits they are.
- Your current credit limits with each creditor.
- Your account balance (total owed) and the payment history associated with each line of credit.
- When you began and closed each of your lines of credit.
- Public records such as bankruptcies, foreclosures, civil suits, etc.
- Other companies that have accessed your credit report in response to applications.

Think of your credit report as your grade card from school. It gives information as to how well you are managing your lines of credit, how well you make payments, and whether there is room for improvement. It is not a reflection of your skills as a person in general, just a reflection of how you have managed your credit lines.

But credit reports are not only used to apply for loans or to grant loans. They can also be used by individuals to monitor their credit. These reports can help you avoid identity theft or to catch it sooner than later if it does happen to you.

What are the benefits of credit reporting?

There are many reasons to check your credit report as often as possible, but not a lot of people know about the benefits. I am going to list some of the reasons why it is useful to check your credit at least once a year.

1.   You get a free credit report each year. It is 100% free! All you have to do is ask for it. A credit report, as seen above, has a lot of details that can help you keep track of your credit rating and your debts. It is wise to make use of the freebie and at least make sure you are up to date on the information listed.

2.   It is a useful and necessary tool in building, rebuilding, or maintaining good credit. It is much more beneficial to know where you stand credit-wise before you consider applying for a new line of credit. Likewise, it also helps you identify things such as identity theft or forgotten debts that have popped back up.

3.   A credit report will be used for important purchases such as a car loan, apartment application, mortgage, and more. Some room rentals even use credit reports now to gauge whether you are a risk or not. You'll want to stay up to date on where you stand especially if you will be needing to move or purchase a car soon.

4.   A credit report can also have errors from time to time. If you are frequently checking and staying informed about what is on your report, then you will be able to catch errors quickly before they affect you. Mistakes can also cause you to have a higher payment on things such as your car insurance. You'll want it to be 100% correct so you don't suffer any consequences from it.

5.   A credit report is often one of the first ways of finding out whether you have been a victim of identity theft. If you see something that is not correct on your report, you can address it sooner. Otherwise, your credit could take years to repair because of someone else's crime.

6.   Just like checking your bank account regularly is important, it is also important to stay

informed on what your credit rating is. It should be an essential part of your financial planning.

How can you obtain copies of your credit reports?

As part of the Fair Credit Reporting Act, consumers are entitled to a free copy of their credit report once every year. There are three main companies that provide credit reports, and each may have a slightly different version so it is best to get copies from all three.

There are three ways you can order your credit report: online, through phone, or by mailing a request.

1. To obtain a free credit report online you will want to go to annualcreditreport.com. This website is the only website that is authorized to fill the requests for free credit reports. It is best to use this site because many websites claim to provide you with a free report but do so as part of a trial membership to their credit monitoring services. Do not give your information to these companies. If you forget to cancel you will be required to pay the fee. The Annual Credit Report website will not ask for any payment information.

2. You can also mail the Annual Credit Report Request form into the Annual Credit Report Request Service to ask for a copy of your credit report. Here is the address:

Annual Credit Report Request Service

P.O. Box 105281

Atlanta, GA 30348-5281

3.   To obtain a copy of your report by phone you can call Annual Credit Report at 1 (877) 322 – 8228.

4.   Alternatively, you can contact the main bureaus and ask for a report. You can do this with all three at the same time or do one at a time. You are entitled to a report from each one time a year. But many people choose to obtain them from the Annual Credit Report website as it includes the details of all the credit bureaus.

Keep in mind that you will be asked to submit certain information to get your report. It is needed to gather your records. You will be asked for your social security number, your date of birth, and your place of residence(s) in the last two years. Many of the companies may ask you other details that only you would know off-hand such as where you worked two years ago or the cost of your car payment. Think of these as added security questions. Each bureau will ask for these details.

What if there are inaccuracies or incomplete information in your credit report?

A recent study done by the Federal Trade Commission showed that about 25% of people were able to find one error on their credit report that could potentially negatively affect them. Credit reporting bureaus are by no means flawless and errors happen often.

The first thing you have to do is find out if the error is your fault in some way. People often find errors associated with different names or nicknames. This is why it is important to use the same information each time you apply for more credit. Use your name as you would your social security number, do not alternate between different versions. Other times there might be errors regarding unclear or missing information on file. If you see accounts missing, ask your creditors to begin reporting your accounts to these bureaus so your report can more accurately reflect your credit, especially if it is positive.

Here are some other common errors or causes of errors:

- Name misspellings.
- Payments may have been applied to incorrect accounts.
- Multiple closed-end lines of credit may make it seem like you have multiple accounts instead of showing as a closed and then later reopened account.
- For those who are divorced verify the debt is all yours.
- Be sure to check for debts that are older than seven years. In that case, they should be removed from your report.

The Fair Credit Reporting Act requires both the company and the informant to correct any errors or to add missing information. If you find that your credit reports have inaccuracies, you must reach out to the credit bureau where the information is listed and tell them the information is correct. You will want to do this in writing. The company then has 30 days to begin an investigation about the information unless they believe the issue is senseless or outlandish. If the information is deemed incorrect, then it will be reported to all three of the main reporting companies so the information can be corrected.

After the investigation, the company is required to provide you with the findings in writing and another free copy of your report if there are changes made. The incorrect information is not allowed back on your file unless a future investigation finds the previous investigation to be mistaken.

Most credit bureaus specify a phone number or address where you can contact them to dispute something on your record.

Now that you have finished this chapter you should be able to understand much of what you see on your credit report when you order it. If you have not ordered a copy in a year, consider ordering one today. What is keeping you from moving forward? It will only take a short amount of time.

Understanding Your Credit Score

All About the FICO Score

You have likely heard the phrase "FICO score" when it came time to apply for a line of credit, a car loan, or an apartment. A credit report offers a detailed history of your credit use and accounts. It also provides you with a FICO score. The FICO score and the credit report are not the same thing, the score is simply a numerical evaluation of the report. The score makes it easier for a lender to gauge quickly what your credit rating is like. The higher the number the better. Many places will also instill a set number for their loaning options. Some won't accept any credit score under 600 for example.

The first credit score was used in 1981 and was introduced by the Fair Isaac Corporation which became known as FICO. There will often be slight variations between your three reports, but there should never be a drastic variation.

Scores influence more than your lending potential. They also can cause changes in your insurance premiums and your interest rates. This is why it is important to work on bettering your credit history and debt issues as it will lead to a higher FICO score.

How are FICO scores calculated?

Your FICO score is a numerical reflection of your credit history. It is calculated using a variety of information from your credit report. Some items will weigh more heavily than others. Let's look at what is used to calculate your score:

1.   Your account history including your payment information. This is by far the most important element in calculating your FICO score which is why it is important to avoid late payments or skipping payments at all costs. Each late payment dings your credit score. This part of your report creates roughly one third or 35% of your credit score.

2.   Use of credit. The general rule to follow is to try to keep your credit lines to only 30% of usage. This will show you have more available than you have due. It is also a good idea to do your best to pay down your debt each month when possible. The highest credit scores tend to have very low usage of their credit lines. This part of the report accounts for slightly less than payment history at about 30%.

3.   How long you have had your lines of credit. The longer the history the better. It shows you can continue to use credit and pay it on time. Shorter credit histories can negatively impact your credit score which is why it is a good idea to try to get a credit card soon out of high school but to treat it as you would cash, only buying what you can afford to pay off each month. This accounts for 15% of your score.

4.   Inquiries and other recent actions. If you have suddenly applied for multiple credit cards this could harm you. Your credit report shows inquiries in the last 26 months. This is why it is important to only apply for what you most want. Also, this includes whether any accounts have gone defunct, been paid off, or have been brought current. Your recent history accounts for 10% of your credit score.

5.   The type of credit you have. If you only have a car payment and a department store line of credit but have the same payment history and such as someone with multiple types of credit, you are likely going to have a slightly lower score. Your FICO score is affected by the variety of

credit you have. If you have many types of loan and you are doing well in managing them, your score jumps up a small amount. Smartly using credit leads naturally to having a variety of credit types. So do not apply for different types of credit if you cannot manage them just to have a variety of credit lines. Make good choices. This is roughly 10% of your score.

The FICO score range:

Your FICO score will range anywhere from 300 up to 850. Some specific types of credit scores can go up to 900, but that is not the everyday case. The higher your number the better your credit report and rating is.

If your credit score is between 300 and 579 you fall into the "very poor" rating level which is about where 16% of the population falls. If your credit score is between 580 and 669 you have "fair" credit and fall where about 18% of the population falls. For those who have a score between 670 and 739, this is considered "good" credit. There are about 21% of US Americans who have "good" credit. A score of 740 to 799 qualifies as "very good" and categorizes approximately 25% of people with a credit score, and anything 800 and above is "exceptional" and constitutes roughly 20% of the population.

The range of numbers will go higher specifically for auto financing, mortgage financing, and bank credit card financing. Each of these have their specific range that relates specifically to the issues that may be faced by those who have those lines of credit.

What is a good FICO score?

Considering the range available for a credit score from 300 to 850, anything above 700 is generally considered good. Most US Americans tend to have between a 600 and a 700 placing them at the higher end of "fair" and the early stages of "good". The FICO scores gives companies a rough estimate of how likely you are to become delinquent on your account. For those who have a "good" credit score, they are reported to have roughly an 8% chance of going delinquent on their account which are very good odds both for the person and the company. Anyone below this category can be an acceptable lending option if they are in the "fair" category, especially on the higher end. But they might not have great interest rates. For those who fall into the "very poor" range, they often have difficulty getting any line of credit or may only be offered credit with outrageous interest rates.

The Importance of a Good Credit Score

Credit makes it possible for you to purchase the things you need or to access things you need such as a home, an apartment, utilities, and a car. Much of these things are too costly to try to purchase outright, especially when it comes to housing. This is when credit comes in hand. It gives people the chance to gain things that will make life easier or more fulfilling without needing to save the entire cost upfront.

A credit score is a part of nearly every single financial transaction that takes place, so it affects how much credit you are given and with what terms you are given credit. Especially when it comes to loans, you could end up paying much more in interest than you would if you'd only had a better credit score. Even if you are someone who does not want to ever finance a car, or open a credit card, you'd be surprised by how many other things rely on a credit score. Utility companies need to see a credit score since they are practically lending a month of services on the basis that you will pay after you use the services. Landlords often check whether or not you are planning on paying cash. Insurance companies often look at credit scores as well. There are also some states in which it is okay for a potential employer to request a part of your credit score and use that as a basis to either hire you or choose another candidate.

The downside of having a low credit score

Having a low credit score can harm you in more than the obvious ways. Not only can it impact whether people lend you lines of credit, but it can affect how much various things cost you. Here are 5 ways negative credit scores can harm you:

1.   A greater interest rate: You won't be offered the same deals as other people, you will likely have a substantial interest rate that can mean you end up paying twice what you borrowed originally depending on how long you take to pay it off, and it can mean things like your car cost a lot more than you hoped.

2.   Your credit or loan applications may not be approved. Not being approved is sometimes a good thing, but more often than not getting a denial when you need credit means your life will be impacted especially if you need it for some type of emergency or need appliances for a new home.

3.   You may have trouble getting an apartment: If you decide you don't want to live with family or roommates, you need a decent credit score to get into an apartment on your own even with a quality income. This could lead to issues like needing a co-signer or having to pay a heftier deposit.

4.   Your utilities may require a large deposit. Though you get the deposit back at the end of your term if you follow through with your terms, it is still an added cost you might not have to front right away. If you are moving into a new home or apartment the last thing you'd want to do is give another couple of hundred dollars to a utility company as a deposit.

5.   You might have difficulty getting a cell phone contract. Cell phones are practically essential in today's world especially given how many jobs need you to be reachable on a near-constant basis. If you do get a contract with low credit you may have to pay for the phone upfront.

What to do if you have no FICO score

Having no FICO score does not mean that you have a 0 score, it's generally not as bad as it seems and it is easy to fix. To have a FICO score your credit report needs to have three different things. 1. You cannot have any mention of being deceased. Occasionally this can happen by accident. 2. You must have a reported account with the credit bureau within the last six months. 3. You need to have had an open account for the last six months or longer.

Just by looking at these three things it can be easy to see how someone might not have a credit score. New adults, for example, might have never had any credit account so they might have a stable income but without any kind of account, they have no score. Anyone who paid off all their debts and closed all their accounts six months ago might no have a score. Thankfully, having no score is an easy fix.

For those who are new to opening lines of credit, it might be wise to apply for a credit card that is secured. Many lenders offer these as a way to begin making payments and establishing credit while being low risk on their end. It will also qualify you for a credit score. If you don't want to open a secured line of credit you can opt-in as a co-applicant for a friend or family member on a credit card or loan. You can also become an authorized user on someone else's credit card. By doing this the lender will likely report the information for both of you to the bureau. These are just a few easy ways to ensure you have a credit score.

How to achieve above a 700 credit score

It's easy to feel overwhelmed when you discover your credit score is not as great as you had hoped. Thankfully, it is fairly easy to raise your credit score with focus and new financial habits. Here are some simple habits to follow and ideas to try to raise your credit score:

1.   Pay your bills on time. As you saw earlier, this is the largest contributing factor to your credit rating. Paying your bills late not only results in late fees, but it also harms your score. Settling on a debt for less than you originally borrowed also negatively impacts you. This doesn't just apply to credit card payments however, you will want to make sure you make all of your payments on time including your loans, rent, and utility bills. If you are behind on any of your payments make it a point to get caught up as soon as possible. This will help boost your score quicker than anything else.

2.   Avoiding applying for new lines of credit or opening new accounts unless you *absolutely* need to. 10% of your score is influenced by the number of inquiries you have had in the last two years. Don't let this 10% be easily swayed because you applied for several cards at the same time.

3.   Lower your overall ratio of amount owed and amount available. If you have used more credit than you have available your credit score will be negatively impacted until you begin lowering this amount. Focus any extra funds you might have on paying down your debt. This will help you increase your credit score quickly.

4.   Dispute any errors you might find on your credit score. Since you are reading this book, I assume you will be following our advice and monitoring your credit report and score. If you see errors, get them handled immediately so they don't negatively impact your credit. A small inconsistency can result in a big credit score boost.

5.   Don't close accounts that are no longer in use. If you paid off a debt let it remain on your report, especially if it is a student loan or

car payment. Showing you paid off a debt will influence your report positively. Also, if you have a line of credit you don't use, do not close the account simply because you don't use it. Leave the line open and you will have a great ratio of money available to money used.

As you can see, a credit score can influence your life in many ways. This is why you must continue with this book and try to follow the advice presented. Improving your credit is like any other skill, it requires attention, time, and energy. If you put in the effort you'll see improvement.

Checking Your Credit Reports and Scores

Once you get a copy of your credit report, it is not enough to simply know your score and history. You have to actively continue to check it and monitor it. If you are in the process of paying down debt or working on bettering your credit score, you might want to consider finding other ways to monitor your credit report outside of the once a year mark. There are numerous ways to keep track of this information and I'm going to share some type of services available for you.

What are credit monitoring services?

Credit monitoring services are a resource that actively keeps track of your credit activity by notifying you of the possibility of fraud, identity theft, and other changes to your credit report and score. It works by actively following your credit report and credit score. People who have experienced identity theft or who fear it often use this service to guard against it. Identity theft can be as minor as a stolen credit card or as large as social security medical fraud. Without these type of services, you might have difficulty noticing when you are experiencing identity theft, especially if you only check your report yearly.

In addition to noticing fraud, credit monitoring services often tell their customers about any other changes to their credit report or score such as inquiries, purchases, and some even offer in-depth tracking of credit scores. These services are a good option for those who are looking to work on their credit and debt and need to stay up to date on their changes. People who lead very busy lives who don't have time to consistently look up their credit scores and credit activity may benefit from these types of services as well.

Types of credit monitoring services

There are some things a credit monitoring service can do for you and other things it can't do. I'm going to explain some of the notices that a credit monitoring service can offer you, and show you how the services can be beneficial.

1. Give you information about new accounts. This is useful in preventing fraud. New accounts do not show up on credit reports until after about six months, but a credit monitoring service can tell you almost immediately. With this

information, you can reach out to the creditor and put a hold on the account. You can also begin the process of filing a report with the police. The best part of this is that you can catch it before any major damage is done.

2.   Name and Address Changes. One very common form of theft is people calling and reporting a lost card and a change of address. In this way, they have a new card sent to them at their address. If you receive notice that you have had your address changed when you haven't moved this could be one of those cases. Again, catching it sooner than later is helpful. Any issues that deal with address changes also have to be reported to the US Postal Office.

3.   Alerts about late or past-due bills. Did you know that it takes seven years to clear a late payment from your credit report? Or that a late payment can push your credit score down by up to 110 points? Credit monitoring services can help you stay up to date on paying your bills. The sooner you catch it the sooner you can be caught up.

4.   Notify you of a bankruptcy alert. These stay on your record for up to ten years, but it is another way that people often commit fraud. If this happens you would have to file with the US Bankruptcy Trustee where the original filing occurred. It's a long process that can wreak a lot of damage if not handled soon.

5.   Suspicious activity. Some credit monitoring services will help by offering suspicious activity monitoring. These types of alerts notify of any strange changes whether in regards to spending finances in a drastically different area than you live in or monitoring money transfers that seem out of the ordinary. This helps catch any strange activity before it gets worse or becomes theft.

How to check your credit score

It's a common misconception that you will automatically get your credit score when you get a copy of your credit report. This is not entirely the case. Credit reports usually do not include your credit score. It's also important to note that you do not have only one credit score. You will have at least three and more if you include the VantageScore (which you will learn about later on). They should similar in range, but will not usually be the same number because they are an estimate based on a series of calculations.

There are a few different ways you can try to access your credit scores. Look to our list for suggestions:

1. Check with your financial institutions. Many loaners such as credit card companies show your credit score as part of your account for free. If your creditors do not offer this, then you might be able to find the information on your online banking. Wells Fargo, for example, updates your credit score online once a month and shows how the number has changed, and what is most influencing the score. It's as easy as logging in to your account and browsing the offered resources.

2. Just like you can order credit reports, you can also order a copy of your score from the three main credit bureaus, and FICO directly. This is a good option if your banking institution does not offer information or you are doing your yearly credit report check.

3.   Some people choose to use credit score services, or free credit monitoring services to keep track of their credit score. Others offer greater resources and protection that charge, but there are many free ones. These are good options for those who are looking to keep track of their credit but don't want to spend the extra money for monitoring or to order directly from FICO.

Hard and Soft Credit Inquiries

A credit check is what a creditor does when they pull up your credit report and your score. There are two main kinds of credit checks. One is called a soft inquiry, and the other is a hard inquiry. The Fair Credit Reporting Act has clear guidelines about the uses of credit reports so thus, doing an inquiry can ding your credit. I'm going to share the key differences between the two:

Soft Inquiry

Most soft inquiries take place without you fully being aware of them. Have you ever gotten an application for a credit card in the mail? Any other "offers" you tend to consider junk mail? If you "pre-qualified" for anything, it is very likely the company did a soft credit inquiry without you even knowing. These offers are sent to anyone who meets a certain level of qualifications.

Another common type of soft inquiry is a background check by potential employers. Some employees like to know the credit of the employees before they hire them to gauge how seriously they take things and whether they are responsible or not.

Checking your credit is also another type of "soft inquiry" that does not negatively impact your credit. This is why it is okay and recommended to check your credit score and report often. It will only help you improve your overall history and score.

Hard Inquiry

These are the kind of checks that will impact your credit score and report. They are also ones that you will know about or should know about. No one can do a hard inquiry without your permission or some kind of engagement on your end whether in the form of an application or signed permission. These occur when you apply for a student loan, other type of loans, car financing, lines of credit, and mortgage. These checks become a part of your report so they are visible to anyone else doing a soft check or a hard check.

Each hard inquiry you do can remove upwards of five points from your credit score.

If, however, you are looking to buy a home and are browsing different mortgage lenders for a variety of rates, all checks within a forty-five day period act as one check and you will not be docked beyond the initial point loss.

Knowing about the types of credit inquiries will help you continue on the path to growing your credit score and making wise choices about how you take on extra credit.

In conclusion

Your credit score and credit report are both essential, but ultimately different things to track and be aware of. Monitoring your credit score and trying to improve it will give you a chance to improve your overall credit report. In the long run, having a higher score will save you money and ease stress should you need to apply for financing or a line of credit.

What is the VantageScore Model?

What is a VantageScore?

The VantageScore was created by the three main credit bureaus and it is used to give an estimate of how likely you are to repay your loaned credit. People use it to gauge trustworthiness and to evaluate overall credit. Vantage score is similar to the FICO score, but there are some key differences we will discuss later on.

VantageScore range explained

Like the FICO score, the VantageScore can range from as low as 300 upwards to 350. Those who have a 300 to 499 for their score fall into the category of "very poor". This accounts for approximately 5% of the population. Those who fall into this category tend not to get approved for credit or most applications. Those who have a score of 500 to 600 are considered "poor". They make up about 21% of the population. They may get approval but it often comes with hefty down payments and very heavy interest rates. Those who have a range of 601 to 640 fall into the "fair" category. This accounts for 13% of people. "Fair" people tend to get approved for credit but they rarely get competitive rates. Those who have a score of 661 to 780 fall into the "good" category. This makes up 38% of people. People who have a "good" score get approved for credit and they tend to get competitive rates. Finally, people with a score of 781to 850 are considered a part of the "excellent" category. They account for 23% of people and they get approved easily for credit. They also tend to get the best deals and rates available.

What is a good VantageScore?

The closer you can get to 850, the better you are in the range of scores. Any score above a 700 is generally considered a good score.

How VantageScore calculates your credit score:

VantageScore may have the same range as the FICO score, but they calculate the score different than the FICO calculations. VantageScore claims not to use exact percentages, but they have given rough estimates of how they calculate the score.

1. The most important factor in your FICO score is your payment history. If you are making your payments on time to all of your accounts this will positively affect you. If you miss payments fairly often and fall behind, or make payments late often, then you will be negatively affected. They usually give a general percentage based on how often you make your payments on time or how often you have missed. It's more of a ratio than a ding based on late payments. Payment history accounts for about 40% of your VantageScore.

2. The next main focus is the type of credit you have and the length of it. VantageScore prioritizes older accounts over many new accounts. It gives lenders a clear idea that you can maintain a line of credit and have a good relationship with the lender. They also like to know that you have a variety of types of accounts such as a car loan, a department store loan, and a credit card versus strictly having car loans, for example. This accounts for roughly 21% of your total score.

3. How much of your credit do you use? VantageScore places value in having more credit available than in use (about 30% in use and 70%

paid off is a good ratio to aim for). Consistently borrowing money or maxing out your credit lines can show you are irresponsible or live on borrowed money. VantageScore calculates credit utilization as about 20% of your VantageScore.

4.   How much do you owe? The amount of your balances both current and past due can influence your VantageScore as well. Lenders like to see that you don't just collect lines of credit for the sake of having a lot available to you, but that you are a responsible person with your credit. If your balances are low on other cards you are more likely to get better rates and funding. This can account for about 11% of your VantageScore.

5.   Inquiries can also affect this score. If you frequently apply for or open new lines of credit this could affect your score. These types of inquiries suggest future financial habits as well. VantageScore uses your recent credit to account for about 5% of your credit score.

6.   How much you have available to you at any given time can also influence your score. Lenders like to know that you only borrow what you need and that you maintain your payments on

it. If you have too much money borrowed, even if you are making monthly payments, you could bring your score down. Total amount borrowed accounts for roughly 3% of your total VantageScore.

The key differences between the FICO and the VantageScore models:

There are some differences between how the two are used and their key features. It is good to know about both the FICO and the VantageScore as each can be used for different scenarios. Let's look at three key differences:

1.   FICO scores require you have an account, as we mentioned earlier, for six months to qualify for a score—this among some other features. VantageScore however, can provide a credit score sooner than FICO. VantageScore requires only one account and one month's history to begin providing a score making it a good option for credit scores for an individual new to gaining credit. So while you may not have a FICO score available to you, you can easily obtain a VantageScore within a month of opening a new account.

2.   Inquiry grouping period: As we mentioned earlier, some hard inquiries can be grouped on your FICO score such as when you are shopping around for mortgage lenders. FICO scores will group these for a total of 45 days. VantageScore groups have a smaller total number of days they will group hard inquiries. The number is only about 15 days. There is a difference however, VantageScore will group all hard inquiries whether it is a credit line, a car loan, and a mortgage check whereas FICO focuses this to only mortgage credit checks.

3.   Another key difference is how the two consider paid off collection accounts. FICO scores will still include all paid off accounts that are over $100 whereas VantageScore will not consider any collection accounts that have been paid off. This helps heal your credit more quickly.

4.   Both accounts give weight to late or missed payments, but FICO scores treat all missed or late payments equally. VantageScore deducts more harshly when the missed or late payments are mortgage payments.

So, as you can see some key differences can easily influence how your score changes and may make one better than the other. The good thing is, for those lenders who check both, they will often use the score that is higher regardless of where it is coming from. But it is still essential and valuable to understand both scores and to know how they are easily changed and influenced by your financial choices.

What Influences Your Credit Rating?

Now that I have gone over some basics in regards to your credit score and credit report, it is time to talk about the biggest mistakes and successes that have the power to influence your credit rating. I will also give you some tips on how to adjust your financial habits to be more successful with each of these categories.

How much weight does payment history hold?

When it comes to our credit ratings, payment history is one of the largest influences on your credit score. As we saw with the FICO score, payment history affects 35% of your score. With VantageScore, it is even higher going up to as much as 40% of your score. If you think about it, this makes absolute sense. Your payment history is probably the most telling fact about your credit history. If you can make the payments on lines of credit you currently have then you are much more likely to be able to make more payments when needed.

Missing a payment or being late can knock a few points off your score even if this only happened one time. So it is extremely important to do your best to make sure you make your payments each month if you are truly focused on raising your credit score and improving your credit report. Also, it is important to know that some payment issues carry a harsher punishment and weight than others. Serious issues such as going to collections, or filing for bankruptcy has the power to damage your credit score and report for up to seven years. This will make it difficult to qualify for many things including new car purchases or a home loan. These situations should be avoided at all costs including repossession, tax liens, and foreclosure.

One way to make sure you don't forget to make your payments is by setting up automatic bill pay. You can even use a budgeting app to remind you when the amount will be removed and how much it was. Automating bill pay will help erase one worry when it comes to finances and make it easier to never miss a payment.

How does credit utilization affect my credit?

The amount of debt or lines of credit you have used, also called credit utilization, influences your credit score and report. Unlike the other aspects, it can both positively and negatively affect your credit rating. How much debt you have affects about 30% of your credit score. This is calculated by the ratio of available lines of credit to used lines of credit. If you have a good deal of credit open and available to you with about less than 30% in use than this can make your credit score higher. The same lines of credit, however, when in use, have the power to bring down your credit score. Always aim to have less than 30% of your lines of credit in use.

To avoid letting this impact your credit in a negative way, begin making a plan to pay down any debts you have. Try to get each line of credit to under 30%. One way to do this is to begin adding a "debt repayment" category to your monthly budget. Use the funds in this category to pay down one debt at a time. When you get to about 30% you can move on to the next one. Some people start with their largest debts and others with the smallest. Do whatever will help you be your most successful self.

It is also important to avoid taking out new lines of credit if you already have a lot borrowed. Adding more open lines of credit will change the ratio but will negatively impact your credit in other ways especially if you have passed due payments or already carry a hefty load of debt.

How does the age of my accounts influence my rating?

Improving your credit score can be done in some simple steps, but there are some techniques and aspects that will take a lot more time to help improve your score. The age of your credit accounts is one example of this. Lenders prefer to see a history of credit accounts that have been established for some time. The older your accounts the more positively they will influence your credit score. This shows that you can continue developing a relationship with one lender and to follow through on the terms of your agreement.

Some people are not aware that closing old accounts or opening new accounts can influence your "average" credit age making your score worse. This is why I suggest keeping lines of credit open even if you barely use the account. Closing accounts too often can suggest that you are more interested in pursuing rewards than you are in building your credit.

I also suggest avoiding opening too many new accounts at one time. If you applied for a car loan, do not run out and get a new credit card alongside it. Opening too many new accounts shows credit lenders that you are trying to take on more debt than you might be able to manage. This aspect of your credit history can affect up to 15% of your overall score.

One way to improve this part of your score is by staying with one line of credit longer than trying to get new accounts. Try to pay down the amount that you have on the oldest account you have and be sure to use it semi-often. Don't put yourself too into debt, but do make it a point to keep your accounts active and open.

What kind of credits should I have?

This is a great question to ask yourself and the answer may vary based on where you are in your life right now. As we mentioned earlier, if you are new to establishing your credit score and credit report, you will want to start small. Focus on a secured credit card, a department store credit card, and/or act as a cosigner for family or someone you are close to. These are three lines of credit that tend to be granted to those with little credit history or no credit history. They do come with risks on your end, but if you make sure to pay down your lines of credit as often as possible and make all of your payments then it can also greatly increase your score.

If you have established credit, but you only have one type of credit for the most part, then it might be time to start adding variety to your credit lines. Aim to have a type of revolving account and an installment account. Your credit can also be increased by having a loan that deals with an asset whether it is a student loan, a car loan, or a personal loan. By adding variety you show lenders that you are financially responsible and intelligent and make wise choices about when and where to borrow money.

Also, by paying down each of these and making your payments on time, you further prove you are a consumer that can be trusted with more credit down the line, thus increasing your overall credit score and credit report. This aspect of your credit report can affect around 10% of your overall rating.

What sorts of things show up in my recent credit history?

Your recent credit history can affect about 10% of your score. This part of your credit report is well connected to other aspects of your credit report. Numerous things will show up in the recent aspect of your score.

Inquiries are one example of what will show up when a lender pulls up your credit report. Each hard inquiry can last on your record for up to two years. It is very important that when you choose to apply to a new line of credit, you take the time to make sure you know where you want to apply to. The more credit inquiries you have the more your score is negatively impacted.

If you have been recently sent to collections, recently missed payments, or recently made a settlement to pay off your debt, then this will also show up on your recent history. These types of choices can affect not only their relevant category but the "recent history" aspect as well.

There are also recent credit history choices that can positively influence your credit rating. If you recently paid off a debt then that will show up on your "recent credit history" as well. This will often boost your credit rating by a noticeable amount.

The only thing you can do to change your recent history credit aspect is to make wise choices and to begin paying off current debts. Instead of applying to multiple lines of credit, only apply to one and make sure you are wise about where you are applying. Instead of trying to pay down all of your debts with smaller payments, focus on trying to pay off one full account as this will show up in your recent history.

The bottom line:

Every financial choice you make has the power to affect your credit report and credit score, but this does not mean you should fear taking out credit or using lines of credit. The power of reading this book and learning about these topics is that you can now make informed decisions. As you move forward and try to increase your credit score, you can focus on the areas that most require your attention. If you are already making your payments on time, then move to the next area, and so on until the only thing you can do is give your accounts time. Each step you take towards improving your score is one step closer than you were yesterday.

What Does Not Affect Your Credit Score

After reading the previous chapters and all the chapters that will follow this, it is common to think that just about everything has the potential to affect your credit score. But in actuality, many things do not affect your credit score. Let's take a look at ten of the things that are commonly believed to affect your credit score, but actually, hold no weight.

1.   Your job and your income. While you do need an income amount to apply for a credit card. Your income itself will not affect your credit score or your credit report. It is merely used to see if you can reasonably make your payments. Your credit reports sometimes include employers but that is only to ensure the report is going to the right person and that there is no identity theft.

2.   Your bank account values do not affect your score. Even if you have a $5 balance, this will not have any bearing on your credit score or your history. Using a debit card as well, even if

it has a visa logo, will not affect your credit score at all.

3.   Your spouse's credit history and score. The only time this will affect you is if you open a joint account and share ownership. Then you are both affected. But if your spouse has terrible credit that will not affect you as credit belongs to the individual, not the family unit.

4.   A late payment of only a few days. While late payments do affect your score once they are reported, they generally are not reported until a couple of weeks after the initial lateness. So you will be charged a fee, but if you make the payment within a set amount of time you are usually okay.

5.   Your assets. Just like your current income and your bank accounts don't affect your credit, neither will any of your assets. They may be used as collateral but nothing that would influence your credit rating or report.

6.   Current interest rates. Whatever you are paying in terms of interest does not affect

whether your score goes up or down. All that matters is how you handle that payment. If you have a high-interest rate on one card the credit bureaus do not care. They simply care if you are going defunct on that loan.

7.   Working with a credit counselor. You will never be harmed for seeking guidance and advice from a credit counselor. It will only work in your benefit if you do.

8.   Being denied credit. The only way this will affect your score is because of the application. If you are denied credit you will not lose points simply because you were denied. While it might hurt your ego, it will not harm your credit history aside from the "hard check" associated with it.

9.   Checking your credit score. It is 100% okay to stay up to date on your credit score and history. Checking will not negatively impact you. If this is a fear of yours you can now begin monitoring your credit more thoroughly now that you know it will not harm your credit in any way.

10.   An Overdraft on your account. The overdraft fee is a pain, but over-drafting your account will not harm your credit score. If you fail to pay back the overdraft or you make a late payment because of it, then your score will suffer. But aside from that, you will be okay if you overdraft your account.

As you can see, there are a lot of mini money mistakes you may have made in the past that have no real bearing on your score or history. So you must focus your energies on what you can do to solve your credit issues or to raise your credit score.

Understanding Credit Cards

In this chapter, I will walk you through the most important information you can know about credit cards. While this is by no means exhaustive, I am going to share just about everything you can know without diving into extensive research. You'll learn about different types of credit cards, what credit cards do for consumers and for the businesses who create them, you will learn about the various benefits they have such as cash advances, their pros, and cons; and we will close the chapter by going over the questions you should ask yourself as you choose what credit cards to apply for, and what credit cards to accept.

How credit cards work (the consumer side of things):

Credit cards are a line of credit issued by the creditor or a major bank. The credit card allows you to spend money that is not cash and is not technically in your possession. In exchange, you agree to pay back the money loaned to you. You can choose to pay back in full sooner or later, but you must make monthly payments to maintain good credit. All credit cards come with associated fees as well. The main fee is the interest charge each month. While some credit cards have zero interest for a short period, that period rarely lasts longer than six months or a year. Interest rates vary in percentage based on your credit score and your credit report. A higher interest rate means you pay the creditor more money over time for the money you "borrowed". The lower the interest rate, the less you pay on top of the loan. In addition to interest rates, many creditors charge fees for late payments, fees for balance transfers, fees for cash advance, and fees for making payments by phone or by mail.

How credit cards work (the business side of things):

Many people struggle to understand how a lender can make money by loaning out money. There is always the question of "what happens if the person doesn't pay back?" or "how does a lender make money if a person pays the account in full each month?". In the case of the latter example, they likely don't make money. But given that billions of people around the world use credit cards, the lenders are bound to make money from someone else's forgetfulness (late payments), someone else's spending habits (interest rates) or each time they do a balance transfer (anyone trying to pay down debt).

The interest rate is likely the way the bank makes the most amount of money. Some interest rates charge as much as 25%. This means that if you borrow $1,000, and you only pay the minimum payment, that means at the end of the year you will have paid an extra $250 in interest alone. Imagine, each year you take longer to pay back the loan you are paying an extra $250. This example is one given with a modest $1,000. Imagine just how much money they could be making off a credit card that has a $5,000 limit and the same interest rate? It's easy to see now how the lender can make their money back and then some.

In addition to charging users of their credit cards, lenders make a percentage of sales from merchants as well. Most merchants want people to have as many payment options as possible as it increases the likelihood of people stopping in. So by charging a Mastercard, for example, Mastercard might charge the merchant .10% of every sale made onto a MasterCard. This might seem minor to the restaurant, but to Mastercard, charging a small fee on every sale means they make a little bit of money back from the money they are lending. What a wise move to make, credit card companies!

Credit Card Versus Lines of Credit

By now you have likely heard the term "credit card" and "line of credit". Some of you might be wondering what the difference is between these two. Knowing what makes them different is key to making the right choices as you decide to take on a credit card or rebuild your credit.

Let's focus on their similarities first. A credit card and a personal line of credit are both (generally) unsecured accounts. Both of these offer a revolving line of credit. You can make a minimum payment or pay your balance off in full. Credit cards and lines of credit both allow you to make purchases, and both allow you the option of cash advances. Both charge interest rates and fees for late payments. It is also important to note that both will affect your credit rating.

Now let us focus on the key differences.

1.   Let's clarify the "generally" parenthetical from earlier. Lines of credit can be secured if you put up a collateral such as your home. But generally speaking, they are unsecured.

2. To even qualify for a line of credit you often have to have proof of an income and documented income whereas most of the time you can apply for a credit card by simply placing your yearly salary. This can make it difficult for someone who has a changing income to apply for a line of credit.

3. Credit cards often offer an introductory low-interest-rate period for purchases. This means you can pay off the debt in full within a certain amount of time and not pay interest. Lines of credit rarely have offers such as these.

4. One of the most important differences to note is how cash advances work in both cases. Lines of credit are used primarily by business because they do not have the very high fees that credit cards have for cash advances. Most of the time, with a credit card, you are unable to take out the full limit of your account in cash. With a line of credit you can take out as much cash within your limit as you need and you do not need to pay a higher associated fee, you simply pay the interest rate like you would any other purchase. This is very useful if an unexpected expense occurs that cannot be charged to a credit card.

5. Credit cards often come with a rewards program, but lines of credit rarely do. This means, if you are going to make a large purchase and have the cash to do so, you should consider putting that large purchase on your credit card so you earn free miles, cashback, or gift cards. Lines of credit do not offer any sort of incentive to use them.

6. Lines of credit typically require a higher credit score and a better credit history than most credit cards. But they can be very useful to have in the event of emergencies.

It is important to know these key differences as picking one or the other or using one or the other will affect how much you pay in associated fees, whether you have any perks, or where you can use it.

All about cash advances

Cash advances are an offering that comes with your credit cards. Typically, a cash advance means you can take out some of your available credit from an ATM, or by forwarding money to a bank or banking system. Cash advances with credit cards come at a steep cost, however.

Typically, the creditor charges a fee just to use the cash advance. Sometimes it can be $10 minimum, other times it can climb as high as $50. In addition to the fee, however, your interest rate is often doubled just to use the cash. This means instead of paying 12.5% interest, you might wind up paying 25% on the amount you requested as a cash advance.

In addition to whatever fees are charged by your creditor, there are often associated fees from the merchant or the ATM just to use the cash advance option. Using the cash advance option is something that should be avoided as much as possible. The fees quickly add up and make it a very expensive loan option when there may be more affordable options available to you.

How does billing and payment work with a credit card?

To understand billing and payment, I want to make sure you understand what a credit card statement might look like. Each month you will receive either an electronic or paper statement for your credit card. The statement will include the following items:

1. Your account balance: This is basically how much you owe your creditor and it includes the amount borrowed and monthly interest charges.

2. Your minimum payment due. You can choose to pay this amount or pay more, but you cannot pay less than this.

3. Your previous purchases: You will be able to see all purchases made in the last quarter or the last month. It will give you the amount of each charge just like you might see on a bank statement.

4. Balance transfers or cash advances: If you have used any of these, they will also be noted on the statement along with associated costs and fees.

5. Fees: Your interest rate and charges will show on your statement. If you've missed a payment or made a payment late, these fees will be on your statement.

6.   Many credit cards now also have a comparison feature where they show how long it will take to pay off your debt if you make the minimum payments and how long it will take if you make larger payments.

Now that you know the main elements of a bill, we can discuss payments as well. So, how is a minimum payment calculated? A minimum payment can go up depending on how much money you have used your credit. The payment is usually calculated at 1% of total owed, and interest. While the minimum is the amount you have to pay (at least) it is very wise to do your best to pay off your debt sooner than later. The longer you take to pay, especially paying at only the minimum payment, the more money you will end up paying to the creditor.

The most important thing, however, regarding billing and payments, is to make sure you pay your bill on time, even if it is only the minimum. A late payment can result in a fee, but not only that, the creditor can also choose to raise your interest rate after just a single missed payment. Also, as we mentioned earlier, your credit score will suffer as well.

Now, here's something people don't understand or know about billing and payments:

your payment does not necessarily go where you'd like it to go. Say for example, that you have taken a cash advance, and you made a purchase with a lower interest rate, and you missed a payment so your interest rate was raised, when you go to make your payment, your minimum payment will automatically be applied to whatever has the lowest interest rate. So while you may think your cash advance high-interest rate will be covered quickly, it definitely will not be if you have a lot of credit used on other items. Anything above the minimum payment, however, will be applied to paying off the highest interest rate. So to pay down that cash advance, you will need to make bigger payments more often.

So, what can you do to make wise choices in regards to billing and payments? Pay your bills on time, pay down debts within the promotional period, pay more than the minimum payment, and avoid cash advances or other choices that cause hefty fees.

Credit Cards: Pros and Cons

Getting a credit card can be very beneficial to your credit score and history, it can also be a useful tool for earning rewards or as an extra option should an emergency arise. The problem is that people don't often know how to use a credit card wisely. I am going to go over some of the major pros and cons of credit cards to help you make the right decision for you.

Pro: They help you improve your credit history and rating when used properly.

Credit cards are a great way to build your credit and show you are a responsible borrower when you use them correctly. This is a great first step for a young adult who is trying to build their credit history for later in life. Each time you make a payment or pay off a debt, your history improves. The longer you stay with a lender, the higher your credit score goes too.

Con: They come with a high cost

We just spent a good deal of time going over the billing aspect of credit cards along with introducing the concept of interest rates early on. Using a credit card can come with a high cost. If used correctly, however, this can also be avoided.

Pro: They are pretty secure

Credit cards can be declared lost. If stolen, you can report it and have it canceled right away and a new card will be sent to you. Fraud investigation teams also help you clear up any theft that might have occurred by having someone steal your credit card numbers. It's pretty easy to see just by checking your account if your information has been stolen or used by someone who is not you. Cash, on the other hand, has none of these benefits. If someone steals your cash there is no way you are getting it back. If you lose it, you can't get a new set of bills. In this way, it is a good way to carry around income.

Con: Credit cards can lead you down the slippery slope of debt.

The problem with credit cards is that people often use them as if they are using cash. They charge what they want to the card, they don't worry about paying it back right away, and instead, think they will pay it back slowly by making minimum payments. This rarely happens, however. Once we fall into debt once, it is a cycle that is difficult to emerge from.

Pro: Reward opportunities

As I briefly touched on in the earlier part of this chapter. Credit cards often come with great rewards that earn you miles or help you get cashback. If you use a credit card wisely, you can wind up saving a great deal of money. Say for example, that you have a set amount of cash for a car. If you buy the car with your credit card instead of using cash, then use the cash to pay off the credit card, you can earn cashback on that pretty much creating your private coupon system. But this is an example of using the rewards system wisely.

Con: Applying for credit cards puts a check on your credit report.

Choosing to apply to a credit card means you are willingly doing a hard check on your credit. As you recall from earlier, hard checks on your credit result in a minor dip in your credit score. Applying for too many credit cards can severely ding your credit over time.

Clearly, there are plenty of reasons to want to avoid credit cards, but also many that show they are a great tool to use. The key to both the cons and the pros is that you need to make wise choices. The benefits of a credit card are only available to those who know how to use them, and the cons only come on when a person foolishly uses their card.

Types of Credit Cards

Now that you know the basics of lines of credit and credit cards, I'm going to introduce you to the variety of credit card types that exist for you to choose form. Some require little to no credit history, others require outstanding credit scores, but there's a nice balance between all of these.

1.   The vanilla credit card: It is just as it sounds, your basic credit card. Typically, it comes with a reasonable interest rate and little to no rewards programs. Like other cards, they have a minimum payment and a revolving line of credit.

2.   Balance transfer cards: These are great options for those who are trying to reduce their overall debt or begin making payments back on their debt. A balance card allows you to transfer over a balance from one or more other credit cards. When you transfer the balance, you also tend to have a zero to low-interest-rate period (usually six months to a year). This means you will have a reduced interest charge which can help you repay your debt more quickly. Some cards have great promotional rates, but good credit helps you access those desired rates.

3.   Rewards credit cards: These are just as they sound, cards that offer a clear rewards program. There are three types of rewards programs typically seen: cashback, points, or miles. The "cash back" type of rewards means as you pay down your debt, you earn a percentage in the form of cash rewards. The points system is similar but usually redeemable in gift cards, miles, or other rewards. Often there will be ways to earn double or triple points. People who travel frequently for business or pleasure enjoy travel rewards as it helps them earn free hotel stays or reduce airfare.

4.   Student credit cards: These are just as they sound, great cards for college students. They generally can only be used by students enrolled in a college or university, they often come with a good rewards program and good promotional rates. They are a good option for students looking to build their credit.

5.   Secured credit cards: These are another great option for someone who is looking to build their credit. Typically, these cards are given to people who pay a security deposit. If the application is approved, the deposit is used as collateral in the event the consumer does not pay

back the credit card. You are expected to make payments as you would with any other card, and your credit improves as you do this.

6.   Subprime credit cards: These are typically geared towards individuals with bad credit. They come with absurd interest rates and often have associated fees that are hard to understand. The terms on the contracts are complicated, but they are offered to almost anyone no questions asked. Avoid these types of cards at all costs.

7.   Limited cards: These are cards that are usually focused on one specific type of store. Gas credit cards are one example or credit cards offered by department stores. They have a minimum payment and generally a fairly reasonable interest rate but often no cash advance.

8.   Prepaid cards: These are not technically credit cards but can be used as such by loading cash onto a card. There are no payments and they do not rebuild your credit in any way.

9. Business credit cards are a great option for those who run a business. They offer a solution to keeping business and personal expenses separate which makes it easier to adjust come tax time. They are only offered to people who have business and require good credit to qualify.

10. Charge credit cards: These are similar to other cards in that they have an amount that can be charged, but they vary in that they have no minimum payment. You must pay the full amount at the end of each month or you will be charged a fee and penalized. Good credit history is usually a requirement for these cards.

Now that you know the types of credit cards available to you, it's time to find out more details about how to select the right card for you.

Factors to consider when picking out a credit card:

As you can see there are many types of credit cards available to you. But aside from knowing which "type" of card you'd like to apply for, there are many other factors you will need to consider. Within each type of card, category are dozens of options for you. Here are some of the most important factors to consider when choosing a credit card:

1.   The APR rate. Also what we refer to as the interest rate. APR stands for Annual Percentage Rate. This is the amount of interest you'll be charged for what you borrow. Many credit cards offer introductory interest rates and then revert to another APR after the period ends. It is important to note that if you miss a payment, your creditor can also choose to raise your APR with advance notice.

2.   Annual fees: There are many credit cards with no annual fees but there are also many that do charge. You'll want to find out if the cards you are considering have an annual fee. Often the fee is offset by a great rewards system, but it will only be worth it if you are making use of the reward system. If you want a basic card that you will only use periodically, it might be best to try to find one that does not have an annual fee attached to the contract. You will also want to look out for other associated fees. How much does the company charge for cash advances in case you need to use it? How much will you be charged if

you accidentally skip a payment? These are all important factors to consider.

3. The rewards program: Is this important to you? What kind of rewards program appeals to you? What do you plan on using the card for primarily? Is a rewards program essential for your card? While this might not be the MOST important factor, it is something to research when window shopping for a new credit card.

4. Credit limit: Depending on why you are getting a credit card, it is important to consider how the limit will influence your choices. If you are getting a starter credit card it is not wise to go for one with a high limit. You will want to train yourself and educate yourself on how to use a credit card. A high limit can be a bad temptation for college students for example. But if you have a business, and you need to be able to make frequent large purchases then you might need the option of a higher limit, even if you pay it down in full quickly.

5. Finally, you might want to ask yourself how you plan on using your card. Will you be making a large purchase and paying it off

slowly, will you be using it for everyday expenses, and then paying it down completely? How you plan on using the card will help you make the right decision.

How to avoid finance charges on your credit card:

Charges on your credit card is just another way of throwing money away. Thankfully, many fees can be avoided with smart planning and wise choices. Let's look at some basic fees and how they can be avoided:

1.   Late fees: These can be charged for missing a payment, and also for paying less than the minimum amount. $35 is the average late fee charge which can sometimes be the cost of a minimum payment itself. If you easily forget to make a payment, consider signing up for autopay. Your payment will automatically be deducted for you.

2.   Cash advance fees: Sometimes a cash advance is very helpful, but they don't come cheap. In addition to the actual fee, you are charged interest. It is best to avoid using this option unless you are okay with paying a hefty

toll. Consider asking friends or family for cash or taking out a personal loan before resorting to this. A loan will often have better interest rates than cash advance on a credit card.

3.   Over limit fees: Many credit cards will automatically decline payments when you try to charge over your limit, but there are also numerous that will not decline. By going over your credit limit, you face an over-limit fee and a larger minimum payment because of it. Know your limit, stick to it, and leave a small gap for when the interest charges kick in. This will help you avoid paying "over-limit" fees.

4.   Interest fees: These are charged monthly after a promotional period ends. You typically pay off your lower interest rate purchases before your higher ones. Avoid paying twice or three times as much as you borrowed by paying your balance in full each month.

In conclusion

Credit cards can be both beneficial and harmful depending on how they are used. There is a lot to learn about credit cards, and it is wise to take the time to familiarize yourself with all the associated concepts before applying for a first or new credit card. Make sure, if you do apply for a new card, that you are choosing the right card for you and your needs. Then you can maximize the benefits of the card.

Scaling the Credit Card Ladder

By now, you have familiarized yourself as much as you can with the basics of all credit cards and the various benefits they can bring. This chapter will continue building on that knowledge but will assist you in developing a plan to better your credit by scaling the credit card ladder. By scaling the credit card ladder you can begin taking advantage of the benefits of various cards and improve your credit score and history.

Now, what exactly does "scaling the credit card ladder" mean? Well, as you will find below each type of card belongs to a "tier" or a step on the ladder. The lower you are on the ladder the fewer benefits you receive as a consumer, on the flip side however, it is also easier to get the card. So, as you start moving towards bettering your credit and improving your options within the credit card system, you will want to try to move up through the tiers. Each tier will be explained below and I'll go into further details about what they each require and how they might help you. Let us begin!

Tier One: Bad credit or no credit options

Student Credit Cards

These do not require much credit history or a high score, but they do require you are a student at a college or university. If you are a student, this is the best place to start. They give you a good stepping stone to make your way up the ladder. They typically have reasonable interest rates. These cards don't require great credit, but typically like to see some type of financial history or income. They are a great starter option and the better of the tier one cards.

Many banks and lenders have a basic student card. They may require a cosigner or some kind of proof of income or have a very small credit limit. Either way, they tend to be easy to get for most students who have little to no credit.

Secure Credit Cards

If you are not a student, then a good first option is the secure credit card. If you recall we talked about these earlier. These are the first rung on the bottom of the ladder. This is where most people begin who either have no credit or who have terrible credit. You need to pay a security deposit to establish this card, and you make minimum payments each month as you would any other card. These credit cards typically ask for $100 - $500 in deposit and offer the same amount as a limit. You don't need good credit or a lengthy credit history to apply as your security deposit guarantees the creditor will be able to pay off what you do not pay off.

Subprime Credit Cards

These are terrible cards with terrible fees and high-interest rates. If you have very bad credit and need to find a way to rebuild your credit, and you don't qualify for the secured or the student cards then you can resort to these, but only do these as a last resort. As we mentioned earlier they often rely on loopholes, sneaky fees, and strange contract stipulations. These cards should not even be considered part of the ladder.

Tier Two: Building credit cards

These cards should have no annual fee. They typically have a nice rewards program that is based on a points system or cashback. The fee is typically reasonable as well. These cards do, however, require credit history and at least a fair credit rating in most cases. Building-credit cards allow you to do just that, build your credit further. They require no deposit and will be the first example of a line of credit that doesn't have a security deposit or relate to your student status.

If you have already established some credit history and your credit rating falls into the "fair" or higher category, it might be time for you to take the leap and sign up for a card with a rewards system. Choose one that has a rewards program that feels beneficial to you, and choose a card that will offer a reasonable limit that won't lead to overspending.

Since Tier Two cards are the most common, and there are so many available to you, I've taken the time to list a few different cards and their basic benefits below:

1. AMEX everyday card. Many people use and love American Express for the many benefits the company offers their cardholders. They have a longer promotional period than most cards (sometimes up to a year and a half) they work on a point system and not just a cashback system, which means you can sometimes earn more points than you would cash which can be redeemed for a variety of rewards.

2. Chase Freedom Unlimited Card: This one also offers an extended introductory period.

They are known for giving out cash bonuses to people who sign up for their cards and accounts, and they offer cashback rewards. Also, Chase Freedom Unlimited has a great offer for cash advance that is unlike many other cards.

3.	Citi Double Cash card is a great choice for those focused on cash rewards. You earn 1% on what you buy and 1% as you pay back your bill. This means you are earning twice what you would with other cards, and you earn as you spend not just as you pay off.

Tier Three: Annual fee cards

While it is a good idea to avoid paying extra fees when you can avoid it. These cards offer rewards programs that outweigh the cost of the annual fee. Some hotels offer these and in exchange for the annual fee they give you a free night's stay in one of their hotels. In this case, the night stay is a better value than the cost of the annual fee.

These are the type of cards that you aim to keep for a long time. They offer rewards programs that make them better to use more often. The annual fee can be anywhere from $50 to $200 and requires a "good" credit score of over 700. Airline cards, hotel cards, major cashback cards all fall into this category. The cost of the fee creates a whole new set of benefits.

These credit cards are not worth having unless you know how to take advantage of the benefits, and unless you can easily afford the annual fee. Choose these cards once you have established your credit and if you have little to no debt.

Tier Four: High annual fee cards

These cards come with great travel rewards, benefits like discounted entertainment options, prestige when traveling, and even things like trip delay coverage. The con, they come with a very high annual fee, usually ranging from $200 to $400. In addition to the high fee, you usually need a credit score of over 730. If you have something slightly lower you can qualify but only with a good income. Occasionally you can get a card with a "fair" credit score, but you will need to provide proof of a very high income.

This is as high as most average people get on the credit ladder. If you get one of these cards then you are doing pretty good in regards to credit. You can use these wisely, earn great rewards, and pay it off monthly or yearly to avoid too high of an interest charge.

Tier Five: High Net Worth Cards

These cards are rarely available to the general public, they are cards that are typically given to big money makers. These cards charge thousands of dollars just to sign up, in addition to thousand-dollar annual fees and are typically only given to people who make over a million dollars yearly. You usually need to have some kind of connection or national prestige to even qualify to apply to these cards.

They come with great perks, and a sense of awe when removed from your wallet, but given that most of us (writer included) are not making millions of dollars yearly, it's probably best to think of the ladder as a four-tier ladder instead of a five-tier ladder.

What to do with this information

Now that you know how the credit card tier system works, it is time to use this information to grow your credit score and history. Figure out where you fall on this ladder and where you want to move towards. If you currently have a second-tier card but want to try to achieve a third-tier card, then look at your financials. What is your credit score? Do you qualify for the third tier card? Do you have debt you need to pay off first?

Also, consider why you might want a card in the next tier? Is it just prestige or are the benefits appealing to you? Whatever the case, make the right choice for you. And now that you have the information handy, you can set new goals and strive to achieve the.

Understanding Business Credit Cards

The last chapter focused on introducing you to the tier system of credit cards. In using the tier system you can rebuild, repair, and grow your finances. Many of those cards are useful for gaining rewards and building your credit, but now we will be looking at another aspect of credit cards: the business credit cards. If you own a business or are in the process of building a business, you will want to know more about these as they will also help you grow your credit and might fill a need you did not realize you had.

What are business credit cards and what makes them different?

The purpose of a business card is basically in the name of its category, it is a card primarily used by individuals to pay for business-related expenses. Both small and large businesses can get business cards including sizes between. Using a business card can help your business build its credit as well. Business cards are similar to regular personal cards in that they often have their rewards program built-in, they require on-time payments and a minimum payment, and they have associated fees that you should try to avoid.

What makes a business card different, first off, is how you use it. For those who run a business, it can be difficult managing finances when all costs are coming out of the same account or being paid with the same cards. In using a business credit card, it becomes a lot easier to manage spending and to organize deductions come tax season. This is especially useful for smaller businesses.

In the same way, your credit can be affected by the use of a personal credit card, business cards can come with a "personal guarantee" which basically states that if you fail to make payments your business credit will suffer, but your credit will suffer as well. If you use a business card it is important to be wise with it. This new card will not be completely separate from you and has both the power to greatly improve your credit and credit history and to break it down quickly. Let's move on and learn more about their advantages, their uses, and the various kinds of business credit cards.

Personal versus Business Cards: Which Should You Choose?

If you are in the process of starting a new business, or have been running a business for a while now and are trying to find a way to more clearly organize your expenses, then it might be time for you to consider getting a new credit card for your business. The next step, however, is to decide whether you want to get a personal credit card and use it just for business expenses, or if you should try to apply for a business credit card. The good think about business cards is that they are open to small or large business. There are some key differences however between a business card and a personal credit card. This section will focus on helping you choose which card to apply for. Here are some factors you need to consider before applying:

1.   Credit limit: Business credit cards tend to have a higher credit limit. Do you need to make frequent big cost purchases? For example, do you tend to charge your inventory and pay it off as you make sales? If you need a larger credit limit it might be a good idea to focus on a business credit card. If you don't need as much of a limit then a personal credit card may be easier to manage. Now, having a larger credit limit does not

mean you necessarily need to be spending that much, but it is something to consider.

2.   Are you trying to build your business credit? Depending on the size of your company, you may be trying to build the credit of your business. A business credit card lender will report all information relevant to your business to the credit bureau. In this case, if you need to build business credit, a business credit card is a better option. Keep in mind though, that the negative information will also affect your credit as well. For example, a missed payment. Often, the lender will report a missed payment for both your business and you personally. If you are not concerned with building business credit, then you don't necessarily need a business card.

3.   Think about your APR needs. Business credit cards are not monitored in the same way personal credit cards are. Because of this, they tend to have higher interest rates, higher fees, and they can change associated interest rates with little notice. If you plan on making large purchases and paying them off slowly (over a year for example) you will likely be paying a lot more in interest rate charges on your business credit card than you would on a personal credit card. If

you plan on making big purchases and almost immediately paying them back (within the month or the grace period) then a business credit card could offer you better bonuses and rewards. This is why it is important to know ahead of time how you plan to use the card.

4.   Consider the kind of rewards and promotional periods you would like. Personal credit cards have outstanding rewards programs. Often you can get cashback on your purchases or earn points that qualify for gift cards or travel perks. Most business cards have a type of point reward system as well. They are usually better than most personal cards, offering bonus points upon signing up, or triple points at select office-type retailers. Also, business credit cards often come with other perks that are related to being a business owner. In some case you might qualify for free wifi with airlines or in certain hotels, sometimes you might even save money at select merchants for having a business card. This, however, will come at a cost. Consider the higher APR. If you'd like to take advantage of these bonuses, you just need to remember that they will only act as bonuses if you are not spending more on your business card in fees than you would on a personal card.

5. Consider your financial future for your business. Are you thinking of getting a small loan eventually for your business? If that is the case, then a business credit card will help you prepare for that. Credit is required to qualify for a small loan, and by using a business credit card before applying, you then begin building credit for your business which will help make the application process easier and more likely to fall in your favor.

Types of Business Credit Cards

There are a variety of business credit cards available for you to apply to. If you have made the choice to go for a business credit over a personal credit card there are other things you should ponder when deciding which card to apply for. Let's take a look at what will help you find the right card for you and your business needs:

1. First, think about whether you want a plain charge card or a business credit card. Credit cards tend to have interest fees associated with them, but as seen earlier, they do come with perks. Charge cards tend to have no clear limit, but the balance must be paid in full each month. If you plan to make large purchases and pay them off

immediately, then a charge card is a better option. You will not pay interest, but you also won't reap the same benefits as a credit card.

Also, just like there are secured credit cards for individuals, there are also secured credit cards available for businesses. This is a good option for those who want to build their business credit and have the money to provide a security deposit. They are often granted to people with low or no credit.

2.   Will you need employee cards? Some companies offer them for an additional charge, but many offer them for free. If you plan on having employee cards it might be a good idea to go with the lender who will be adding these as a bonus on your account instead of charging you. If you only need one other employee card then you might be okay with a company that charges for them, but as always, weigh out the costs for both arguments and go with what will result in a better deal for your pocket.

3.   Consider where your business spends the most amount of money. Many business cards come with perks and rewards programs that earn double, triple, or more points in specific

categories. When choosing a card, go with the one that rewards your business spending habits the best. Do you frequently travel? Then it might be better to go with a card that offers free miles or bonus points for travel purchases than say going for a card that has dining rewards. A credit card with points given for gas might be great for you if your business requires you to travel by car frequently. If you tend to spend sporadically never really having a clear pattern, then a plain cash-back rewards program might be best for you as each purchase you make will help boost your bonuses.

4.   What other bonuses are you looking for? When you first get a card you will often be given a promotional interest rate or some other kind of bonus. You will want to think about the above when deciding which bonus will most benefit you. For example, some cards offer a 0% interest rate for the first 15 months. This might be important to you if you need to make a large purchase that you would rather pay off slowly, such as laptops, printers, or office equipment. Other cards offer multiple points based on how much you spend in the first year. If you plan on making large purchases, but know you will pay them off fairly quickly than the bonus points may

be a better offer for you than a longer 0% interest rate.

5.   Do you need special protections? Some cards that have a higher annual fee but will offer you protections such as purchase insurance, travel assistance, extended warranties or more. If the cost of these potential worst-case scenarios worries you more than the annual fee, then you might want to find a card that offers these types of protections. Be sure to ask as you do your research.

Some people compare their card options before applying by creating excel spreadsheets or creating a chart in a notebook. If you are having difficulty narrowing down which card to apply to, creating a guide like this might be helpful for you. Either way, be sure to do your research. Don't apply to just any card, and don't apply to every card.

How to get a business credit card:

Most people don't realize how many individuals qualify for business cards. Numerous categories qualify for a small business credit card. Anyone who tutors or babysits and charges money for it. Anyone who has a side gig like Uber. If you're a freelancer, you also qualify. People who sell items at craft fairs or farmers markets. People who sell books on eBay, people who sell through Etsy or Shopify. It isn't even a requirement to be making money from a business. If you have an intent to make money doing something like this soon, then you still qualify to apply. Now, while most people might qualify to apply, the application process is different than that of personal credit cards. I'm going to guide you through the application process so you have an idea if it is something you'd like to try out.

1.   You will need a legal name for your business. Whatever name you use to do business, is what you will want to put here. If you have a small company with a registered business name you can use that, otherwise if you freelance or make money under your name, just put your legal name as the name of your business.

2.   A tax identification number. Once again, this number will vary based on whether you have a registered business or not. For those who have a business or an LLC, you will want to use your Employer Identification Number. For those who are applying under their legal name, it is

better to use your social security number unless you also have an Employer Identification Number.

3.   The type of business you run. For those who are an LLC, you will select cooperation or partnership depending on how you've registered your business. For those working for themselves, you will label yourself as sole proprietorship.

4.   What industry you are involved with. There is usually a long list to choose from. It does not need to be exact, but choose the option that most closely aligns with what you do.

5.   What your role is in the business. This is easy for those who provide services like freelancers—you are your own boss. For those who have a business setup, you'll have to create a role for yourself. Are you the "owner", the "manager" or the "president" whatever label you chose, just be sure you use that label normally.

6.   The length of your business. As I mentioned, you can apply before you exist as a business. In that case, you will just put 0 for 0

years. If you have existed for some time, let them know how long you have been in business in years.

7.   Estimated monthly expenses. This is not found on each application, but many lenders want to know about how much you anticipate spending on your card monthly. This will help them decide on the limit and whether to approve you.

8.   Your personal details. Just like you would on a personal credit card application, you will need to provide personal details such as your address, full name, phone number, birth date, social security number, and more.

What you need to secure a quick approval:

So, while the application process may seem lengthier for a business credit card and a personal credit card, it does not mean that it is much more difficult to get approved. There are keys to getting approved and much of it involves proper preparation. I'm going to guide you through what it takes to secure a quick approval.

1.   Good credit: It does not need to be excellent or very good, but you need good credit. If you have already established credit for your business then you'll want to do your best to make sure it is in the "good" category. If you have yet to establish credit for your business, then the application will rely on your credit. Before you decide to apply for a business credit card, do what you can to make sure you have set yourself up for success by improving your credit history and score.

2.   Be prepared to sign a personal guarantee. This is a document that states that if your business does not pay back the debt then you personally will be held responsible for the debt. If you fail to make payments on your business card, this guarantee states that the bank is legally allowed to take the loan from you personally, even if the business is a separate entity.

3.   Avoid lying in the hopes of being approved. A business credit card application process typically involves a variety of questions. Do not lie in the hopes that you will qualify or get better benefits. Often, when in the process of the application, the lender may call and ask you more questions about your business. You should answer

these honestly. If your business has yet to make money, explain how much you anticipate making and why. Explain why you believe a credit card for your business will help you. Oftentimes if your reason is valid, the lender is more likely to approve you even if you are only granted a smaller limit.

4.   Try to go where you have already established a relationship. If possible, work with a bank you have history with. If you have already established yourself as a good lender with one company they will likely try to make the deal happen because you have been a loyal customer.

What transactions could the business credit card be used for?

There are numerous cases when a business credit card can be used! Using the business credit card over cash or your personal accounts will help you come tax season when you begin to create a list of deductions. Let's take a look at this extensive list of possible charges you can place on your business credit card:

1.   Office equipment: If you have a home office, or you use office equipment to help run your business you will want to charge this on

your credit card. Computer purchases, even if you use them for business and personal reasons, printers, desks, office chairs all count. Also, you can include stationery, office supplies, and any tools you use to do your work: digital tables, keyboards, cameras, etc.

2.   Fees, dues, and subscriptions. If you are part of a membership that helps your business, or you pay fees to do your work (being part of a website that charges for example) or you receive magazines or journals that help you run your business, these can be deducted and thus should be charged on your business credit card.

3.   Conferences and travel: If you have to travel for work, and only for work, then you should charge that on your business card. This includes traveling to work with clients, traveling for conferences or fairs, or traveling for sales. Put this on your business card.

4.   Advertising, marketing, and promotion. If you take out an ad, pay for promotions on websites, or any other kind of business-related promotions (Facebook ads count as well) then pay for this with your credit card.

5.   Education: Do you plan on taking a class in the field you work in? Are you part of a subscription service that helps you grow in your career (Skillshare, Masterclass for example) then you should be putting these on your charge account to help you later on when it comes time for deductions.

6.   Mileage: Anytime you travel for work and pay for gas, put that on your business credit card to help you keep track of it.

7.   Insurance: If you pay for additional insurance that benefits your business, you might be able to put this on your business credit card.

This list is by no means the only list of things that should be charged on to your business credit card, it is simply a list of ideas to get you thinking about how and when to use your business credit card. Each time you are about to make a purchase, consider if it relates to your business in some clear and provable way. If so, then proceed with our business card, especially if you have the cash to pay it off before the end of the month.

Using the business credit card will help you figure out how much you are spending to run your business and will help you when it comes time to deciding your rates, or what you will charge for your products.

Now that we have reached the end of this chapter you have what you need to help you decide whether you should apply for a business credit card, what kind of credit card you should seek out, and how to apply and use a business credit card.

What Is A Credit Card Balance Transfer?

We discussed balance transfer cards early on. These are a credit card where you transfer one or more of your credit card debts. There is usually a fee associated, but you'll be given a promotional period in which to pay off your debt. This usually ends up saving you a great deal of money. If you pay $75 in interest on one card each month, but you plan on paying off the debt within a year, for example, with a balance transfer card you could be saving almost a thousand dollars on the interest charges alone. Let's take a closer look at these specific type of credit cards.

Balance transfer in a nutshell

Balance transfer cards are a great resource if you are paying multiple credit card debts, or paying debts that have a high-interest rate. The key to balance transfer cards, however, is to use them wisely and lower your debt as much as possible within the promotional period. Basically, you use one card to pay off the debt that exists on another card but you save on interest charges for the entirety of the promotional period.

Once you are approved for a balance transfer card, the creditor will begin the process of transferring your balances to the card. The amount you are approved is the amount you can transfer. In some cases, you might not be able to transfer the whole of your debt.

The application process for a balance transfer card works roughly the same as a regular personal credit card application. You'll provide your basic information, share details about your income, and you will receive a hard credit check. Once you are approved you will be given a credit limit and you can decide whether to transfer all of your debts or only some of them.

The balance transfers take a few weeks to sort out so you will usually have to continue making payments for another month until all the transfers are complete. You usually have to go with a different company. You cannot transfer a balance from one Citi card to another Citi card for example.

When should you do a balance transfer?

The option to do a balance transfer very well could help you reduce some of your credit card. While this can be a great option for those who have a mid-level amount of credit card debt, there are also times when it is not as beneficial to do a balance transfer. Let's take a look at some cases when it is good to do a balance transfer and when it might not be as helpful.

1.   It is helpful If you have positive credit. You actually need a decent credit score in order to qualify for a balance transfer. This will likely not be the case if you have missed payments, have done late payments, or are completely maxed out on many different accounts. Some popular balance transfer cards, for example, require a credit score of over 700. Chances are if your score falls in the poor category, you might be better off figuring out a debt repayment plan and focusing on that until you improve your score enough to get a balance transfer.

2.   If your debt is very high it might be a good idea to hold off. While a balance transfer can help to reduce your overall debt, it won't do much if you are already burdened by your debt and have no way to make extra payments beyond the minimum payment. The goal of using a balance transfer card is to pay off or mostly pay off the debt within the promotional period. If you end up going into the non-promotional interest rate, it might actually be more damaging than good. It

will also give you even more credit you can use if you feel desperate enough to use it because of your situation. Avoid it if you have a high amount of debt and are struggling to make the minimum payments.

3.   If your debt is close to being paid off then do not do a balance transfer. It is important to remember that balance transfers each come with an associated fee. If you are close to paying off your debt, you will still have to pay that fee. You might not save as much money as you would if you just focused on paying off the debt within the year you had planned on paying it off. Also, a few paid down accounts is better for your credit than one paid down balance transfer.

4.   If you are trying to transfer balances from some of the same companies avoid the balance transfer. Many people are not aware, but you cannot transfer balances from the same company to a new card, nor can you transfer more than one balance from a company. A lot of the time lenders leave off this detail in their offer until the person has been approved. It is one way to bring in new customers.

If you have no intention of paying it off, or you plan on only ever making minimum payments, then just hold off. Some people attempt to use balance transfers simply as a way to buy themselves time, but in the end, this will harm your credit more than it will help it. It's important to only use the balance transfer when you know you can pay more than the minimum payment. Or when you know you will pay down the debt a lot sooner. Then it is worth saving extra on interest.

Pros and Cons of balance transfers:

As we discussed earlier there are a lot of benefits to balance transfers, but they can also come with many costs. Let's take a look at the pros and cons of utilizing the balance transfer features on new credit cards:

Pro: It makes it easy to make payments.

One key feature of balance transfers is that instead of making many payments to different lenders, you end up paying only one payment. Once you transfer all of your balances you will have a new minimum payment that must be made on the whole of your debts. This is good for those who are looking for an easier way to manage paying down their debt.

Con: There are balance transfer fees you must pay.

Even if you pay off your debt in the promotional period, you will still be charged a fee. The key is to weigh the cost of the fee versus the amount you will save on your interest charges before deciding to proceed. Most of the time the fee you pay is a percentage of about 3% to 5% but it varies with each creditor. If you are transferring a balance of $10,000 that means you could wind up paying $30 or $50 in addition to the debt. But this is often substantially less than you would pay in interest charges.

Pro: You save on interest charges!

This is probably the number one reason people sign up for a balance transfer. The promotional period is the amount of time you will be able to make payments without being charged interest. Even if you don't manage to pay off the whole of your debt, if the interest rate s lower on the balance transfer than it is on the credit cards you had open, then you will still wind up saving more on interest charges, and you will bring down your debt.

Con: You won't get the low APR for the entirety of your contract.

The promotional period is likely why you are considering a balance transfer card. It is important to keep in mind that this will not last past the period. Sometimes the interest rate is lower than your current lender, but often the card won't have much greater of an interest rate because your credit is likely not much better than it was when you applied to the original lender.

Securing Your Credit

How identity theft can ruin your credit

In 2017, near seventeen million people were affected by identity theft alone. Identity theft can range in severity from only a few simple transactions, to whole accounts being created in your name. One woman from Washington was charged with multiple accounts of identity fraud. One of her victims had his credit score ruined after she opened nine different accounts in his name. It is a very serious issue that has the ability to ruin your credit tremendously and to make it very difficult to repair. People can easily steal our identities just by having one tiny detail from our records. Something as simple as a date of birth, or a random guess at your social security number, or your home address has the ability to gain them new credit cards, personal loans, cell service, and other utilities and credit accounts. Not only that, but people who steal identities often resell them on the black market which only means that your information might be at risk of being used again in the future. Every time you fill out a form, apply for something, give details over the phone, you are at risk of having your information stolen and used for someone else's gain.

When your identity is stolen and used to give the thief money, there is no incentive for them to pay it back. There is no incentive for them not to apply to as many accounts as possible or use whatever they can! It is also extremely difficult to actually find out the real identity of the person who stole your identity most of the time. By the time you realize your identity has been stolen, it is near impossible to do anything about the effects it has on your credit score and credit history. If you do file reports and try to dispute the scores and history, it can take months for any of it to work out in your favor.

Identity theft can damage your credit score and history in many ways. Let us look now at a small list of all the damages identity theft can cause.

1.   Damage to your payment history. If a thief opens up a new line of credit in your name, and you do not catch it immediately, chances are that a missed payment or a late payment is going to happen with these new accounts. As you learned earlier, a missed payment or a late payment has the potential to ding your credit score by many points. With each missed payment the amount of points deducted increase. Even if the card is reported as stolen, the payments are still in

your name and under your information. This means that your credit score will suffer in the time it takes to try to figure out what is happening and while trying to fix it.

2.	If the thief fails to pay and you are unaware, the debt will be turned over to collections. A collections notice is much more damaging than a missed payment or a late payment. Chances are, that if you are already oblivious to the identity fraud taking place, you might not be aware of these new accounts that are not being paid on. The lender, also, has no way of knowing that it is not you who is failing to make the payments. So, they then move forward with collections. Then, on top of the stress of identity fraud, you have the added stress of having to track the collections from seller to seller as they are sold and resold.

3.	The thief will likely take the card or account and spend as much money on it as they possibly can before they are caught, or the account is frozen. The odds of the thief doing this are extremely high, unless they are caught before it happens. If your debt goes from a small 30% percent to 70% or more utilization, this has the potential to bring your FICO score down by as much as 40 points. Thieves know that the card will likely close down very soon, so they do their best to spend as much of it as possible and as quickly as possible. Even if you freeze the holds, get the situation investigated, you will still have this utilization on record until everything is cleared in your favor. Even after an investigation, it is difficult to clear things from your record.

4.   If you remember from earlier, length of credit accounts also has the ability to affect roughly 15% of your credit score. When someone gets your information, they will often try to open more than one account in your name. If they open more than one account, this reduces your average account length and also lowers your credit score as a result. One new account may not reduce your account length percentage, but one new account in addition to any new accounts you have opened, or if the thief opens more than one account, can bring down your score by many points.

5.   Each inquiry has the potential to damage your credit score. If the thief has your information, they are likely not running "soft" credit checks. It is likely they are applying to as much as possible which equates to multiple hard checks on your credit card. Remember from

earlier, that FICO scores do not group credit applications together in a single period, only mortgage applications. While the thief may not always be able to open multiple accounts in your name, they will likely try to open as many accounts as possible. With each application comes another ding to your report and your credit score. Each time you are denied as well, you lose credibility.

Getting your identity stolen, as you can see, has the power to greatly affect your credit report and score. While it is clearly not the worst thing that can happen to anyone, it is something that can cause a lot of damage and make it difficult to repair. As we move on in this chapter, we will focus on ways to prevent identity theft, and what you can do if you find that your identity has been stolen.

Ways to Avoid Becoming an Identity Theft Victim

With the prevalence of online shopping, fake websites, phone scammers, email scammers, and door to door sellers, it is easy to see how people can become a victim of identity theft fairly easily. There is also the threat of having information stolen by hackers, having people take information by eavesdropping as you fill out a form, or through wi-fi. Everywhere you turn there is a new threat to your information. The good news, however, is that there are many ways that you can also reduce the possibility of having your information taken. We're going to look at some easy to follow steps to helping prevent you from becoming an identity theft victim.

1.   Do not give out your information to just anyone. There are a lot of people who know how to make themselves sound or read as professional. Many people pretend to be your credit card or service provider and will call, then ask for your information to "verify" your account. They will then use that information to steal your identity. The best way to avoid this is to be cautious with who and where you give out your information. If someone calls you claiming to be from a bank, deny giving them information. Hang up and actually call your bank and ask to speak to customer service. This is not only limited to phone either. People have been able to send mass text messages, create deceiving websites, or send emails with the sole purpose of scamming you. Always be cautious when you're being asked to verify by providing your information. Especially if you were not the one to initiate the contact.

2.   Avoid clicking on links you are unsure about. At the time of writing this book there is a mass virus spreading through Facebook messenger. It begins with the text "is this you in this video?" and then provides a link to said video. Once you click on the link your messenger has the virus and begins sending it to everyone on your message list. All because of one click. The same can happen with identity theft. It is incredibly important that you do not click on links sent through email or text message when they are from senders you do not know.

3.   Shred your important documents. Many people who steal others' identities often go digging through trash for things like pre-approved credit card offers, bills with personal information, and other similar documents. It is important to shred anything that might have very important information on it to help avoid giving anyone easy access to your personal documents.

4.   Do not carry important documents around like your social security card. There is no need to. There are very few instances in which you need the actual card with you, most of the time you just need access to the number. Memorize the

number and stash the card away in an important space.

5.	Also, only carry around the cards you absolutely need to carry. Keep cards you do not use tucked away in a safe spot. It helps keep you from accidentally losing them. A lost card can still be used until you shut it off.

6.	Protect your mailbox! Theft from mailboxes happens commonly around tax return season when people are expecting checks in the mail. Around Christmas season, a lot of people also find their packages stolen from their front doors. To avoid this consider having items delivered to a safer location, like your work, or a family member's home if they are home more often. If possible, get a lock for your mailbox.

7.	Monitor your online accounts. Oftentimes you can have notifications sent to your cell phone if someone logs in from a new location, or if someone requests a new password. If you have not set up notifications, it's easy to do. You can also get notifications for checking accounts when you run low on funds, or when you get close to your limit on credit cards. That way, if someone uses your card, you can report it before you get to zero.

8.   Create very strong passwords. Do not use full names of people you love or birthdates. Don't use single word passwords, instead try to create passwords that incorporate, letters, symbols, and numbers. Try to think of passwords that would be impossible to guess simply by having some of your information. Many devices or websites also have a "suggested password" feature which helps you create difficult to guess passwords.

9.   Turn on the bonus authentication feature. If your banking, creditors, or other secure websites ask if you want to turn on the two-factor authentication, use it. Often this means that you have to add information like a second email address or a phone in addition to the email address. Sometimes it just might ask for a password and an answer to a security question. This is a bonus feature that helps add an extra level of security to your account and you should use it to your advantage.

10.   Avoid public WIFI. Some hackers know how to create their own networks as a way to get people to browse on their network. They can then monitor the individual's use and steal information like login info. Avoid using public WIFI that is not secure and don't log on to banking or creditor accounts while on public WIFI.

11.   Check your credit report frequently. This will help you stay up to date on the information that is appearing on your credit report and affecting your credit score. If you want to avoid paying for a credit report, consider spreading your three free reports out so you have access to one every four months.

12.   Destroy old cards. If your card has expired, don't just throw it away. Do not keep old cards lying around either. Old cards, expired or not, can be used to reach your bank account or creditor so that the thief can get access to new cards.

13.   When shopping online be sure to only use trusted websites. Be sure to look at the web address to help you see if it is a secure website. It should have an "HTTPS" not "HTTP"

only. If it is HTTP only then the website is not secure and may be easy to hack into putting your information at risk of being stolen.

14.   Stay up to date on the latest forms of identity theft. Read about the latest hoaxes, the latest viruses, etc. Do not assume you know it all. By learning about the new ways people are accessing information then you will be able to stay one step ahead and protect yourself in more ways than before.

15.   Consider Identity Theft Protection. If you have great credit, and you have the extra space in your budget, consider signing up for identity theft protection. Credit monitoring services often catch identity theft much sooner than any other method of monitoring. Some even notify you within hours of someone applying for a card under your name. These alerts will help you stay on top of your credit score and history.

16.   Stop your mail if you will be gone for days and do not have a key. Placing a hold on your mail is easy to do. Be sure to take this step if you plan on being away for a while and do not have a

lock on your mailbox. It will help you avoid giving access to important mail to thieves.

17.   Contact your billing companies if you notice a statement or bill is late. There should be no reason for them to arrive later than usual, or by more than a day or two late. If you notice statements are arriving late then reach out and ask why.

18.   Be careful of what you post on social media and keep your accounts limited to people you know. Many people take countless casual photos daily, but you need to be careful about how much information you post online. If you frequently post birthdates that you use as passwords, then that can make it easier for a thief to guess your information. Likewise, be sure you don't have an ID or a credit card in the background of a photo. It's very easy to zoom in and take the numbers.

Many of these steps are easy to follow. If you have not been doing any of the above now is a good time to start. For those who are parents, it is also a good idea to pass these habits on to your children to help safeguard their identities later on in life.

What to do if you find you are a victim of identity theft

Finding out you have been a victim of identity theft is crushing news. You know you are in for a whirlwind of problem solving. It does not have to make you completely hopeless, however. Recovering from identity theft is possible. If you find out you are the victim of this crime, I'll guide you through the necessary steps to reclaiming your credit and solving this problem. Let's have a look:

1.   Reach out to the lenders or banks where you know there are new accounts. The important thing to do first is to put a hold on those accounts and to let them know there has been fraud. They can then begin problem solving on their end right away as well.

2.   Make sure to reach out to one of the main credit reporting agencies. Once you reach out to one, they are legally obligated to share the information to the other agencies. This saves you some time in a stressful moment. If you would like to however, you can reach out to each one, so they are aware as soon as possible. You will also want

to have them put you on "fraud alert". For a year after beginning this, no account will be able to be open without additional screening. It will become harder for anyone who has your information to use it to open new accounts. You also have the option to extend this beyond the year mark for an additional cost.

3.   Ask for a credit report. After reporting the fraud, you can ask for your free credit report. This way you can find all the details possible about any other existing accounts or applications being processed. It will also help you find out how much damage was done and how quickly. You will want to get them more often than the yearly mark if this has happened to you.

4.   Freeze your credit account. This will make it so that no one will be given access to your credit history without you giving clear approval. It will make it difficult for any new applications to be processed and will add an extra layer of security to your credit for some time after the fraud incident.

5.   Be sure to contact the creditors and loan companies again and request copies of all related documents. You can be given copies of the application which will help as you begin filing your fraud case. You'll also want to gather relevant information from your own personal accounts to prove that it is indeed fraud.

6.   Likewise, you can also ask any debt collectors for information regarding your debt if the identity fraud went as far as being a "collected" debt. This will help you understand how much damage has been done and to form your case more strongly.

7.   After your fraud report has started, you will also want to contact the lenders and debt collectors (if applicable) and let them know that you wish for them to stop reporting the information to the credit bureaus. You will need to provide a copy of your fraud report, but this will at least help stop the reporting from further damaging your history and credit score.

8.   Contact your local police force. You will want to file a police report that includes all of the information regarding the fraudulent activity, anything related to your identity being stolen, and a copy of the fraud alert. After filing the police report be sure to also collect a copy of the report for your own records.

9.   Contact the IRS as well. If someone has your information, they may try to file a fake tax return with a different address in the hopes that they can obtain your tax return. Contacting the IRS will help you avoid all of this. The IRS should also know about all fraud in the event they need to do an audit in the future.

10.   Reach out to your health insurance company. This does not happen as often as people creating accounts, but occasionally someone might use your information to receive medical benefits. This could hard your fraud report so you will want to make sure that no one is receiving benefits by contacting your insurance company and letting them know that you have been a victim of identity theft.

11.   Then you will also want to contact the DMV. Someone could easily use your ID for other types of fraudulent activity so you will want to make sure no other IDs were ordered and sent anywhere, or that no one has taken your name and registered new addresses or new plates. Letting the DMV know will help you avoid any possible related issues and help create a clearer case.

12.   Finally, take the time to work on your login information, clear your accounts, and check in with all of your true creditors. Check in with your utility company, change your login details with your bank, keep track of your savings account or other credit card accounts that truly belong to you. Make sure you do your best to make it so that the current thief cannot access your information again as easily.

As you can see, fixing the issue of identity theft is not easy by any means. It requires an extensive amount of time reaching out to certain companies and parties. If this happens to you it will be very stressful and could make it hard to recover from. That is why it is important to follow the earlier guidance and to do all that you can to avoid becoming a victim to identity theft. Sometimes, even by following this guidance, you might still become a victim. But it is much harder to let damage happen if you are consistently checking your credit score, your credit report, and staying up to date on your accounts. If anything looks suspicious report it right away. If possible, sign up for a credit monitoring agency if it is in your budget and you have good credit.

Strategies for Credit Repair

Now that you fully understand the basics of credit cards, credit scores, and credit reports, you might be asking yourself, "But how do I fix my credit if it is poor or fair?". Well this chapter is going to focus on providing you with steps to address your bad credit score and history and giving advice on how you can improve it. Here are easy to follow steps that you can do to improve your credit score and clean up your credit report.

1.   **Pay your bills on time.** This is probably the easiest way to boost your credit score. We mentioned earlier how damaging it can be each time that you do not pay on time. If you are behind on payments, get caught up right away. If you have been paying your bills on time, continue doing that so you can continue improving your score. Late payments can remain on your history for up to seven years. So do not let that happen. Fix this if it is an issue right away to see a boost in your score. If it helps, consider setting up automatic bill pay so that you do not have to remember when each bill is due. Some people choose to pay all the bills for a pay period when they get paid, even if it is not due yet. This also

has the added bonus of helping you avoid using money that is meant to go towards paying your bills.

2.   **Start paying down your debt, or if it is already getting lower, do not use your debt.** The goal is to try to keep your debt usage to only about 1/3 of actual available. If you have debts that are maxed out or near maxed out, it is time to put those cards away and to stop spending on the accounts. Your credit score will not improve in this area if you continue using them. Reducing your overall credit utilization has the power to bring your score up by a noticeable amount quickly. So, make a debt repayment plan and focus on paying down those loans. If it helps, cut up your credit cards. Some people also freeze them, literally in tubs of water. Whatever will keep you from spending, do that. It you need to, give them to a trusted friend or family member who will not use them and will keep you from using them. If you do not have the cash to pay for something you should not be spending that money on your credit account. Especially if your utilization is already very high.

3.   **Keep track of your credit score and frequently check your credit reports.** If you are going to focus on repairing your credit history and credit score, then it is time for you to order some credit reports and to begin tracking your credit score. You will want to know exactly who and where you own money in order to pay it down in the right way. Ordering a credit report is not only about having access to the creditor information, it is also to ensure there are no inconsistencies. If you see an error on your credit report, you need to report it to the bureau right away. A large amount of people find errors on their report each year, with most of them being errors that are capable of harming their score in a noticeable way. If you see an error, fix it right away in order to see a boost in your credit score quickly.

4.   **Serve as a cosigner for people on other loans.** If you are ready to begin rebuilding your credit and you have already been making your payments on time and are working on bringing down your overall credit, you can sign up as a cosigner for someone else's account. If you recall, being on someone else's account also affects your own credit. This can be both good and bad, so only do it with someone you trust. If you know they will be paying the bills on time, this has

the potential to benefit your credit score by improving your credit history. However, do make sure it is someone you trust. If you do not think they will make the payments it is more of a risk than a benefit.

5. **Apply for a secured credit card.** Take a small chunk of money and use it as a deposit towards a secured credit card. Secured credit cards are an easy way to open a new type of credit, to improve your payment history, and to do so without fear of temptation. The reporting that comes with a secured credit card will impact your report and score in a positive way without putting you at risk for overspending. Using a secured credit card feels more like using your own money so you will be more careful with it. These are easy to apply for and many are approved even with no to low credit.

6. **Get a loan specifically for building credit.** Many credit unions offer these, and you might be able to find them at community banks as well. These types of loans work in the same way that secured credit cards work. You take out a loan against a deposit you provide, and you make payments. Your payments are reported, and they help to slowly rebuild your credit. It's a good

option if you have enough to provide a deposit and you need to balance out the payment history part of your credit report.

7. **Become an additional user on someone else's card.** You can do this without ever actually using the card. Just by being added on to someone else's account, you benefit from their monthly payments being made. If the person is okay with you using the card, they can also set a limit on how much you spend in the event the whole amount is too tempting. This is one easy way that you can build your credit without taking out any loans or placing any deposits.

Rebuilding your credit is a long process, but that does not mean that you cannot do anything about it right now. As you can see from our seven easy steps above, many of these are things you can do in a single day (check your credit report for example) and others are small, easy changes you can make with the help of a trusted friend or family member.

As you work towards building your credit score and credit history, the most important thing is that you make wise choices going forward. None of these tips will be helpful if you continue making damaging choices with your credit such as taking out more loans than you can handle or making late payments. Follow common advice for healthy financial habits and use them to your advantage. Once you rebuild your credit score and get into the "good" category. You will be able to start qualifying for more items. This is when you can focus on "scaling the credit card ladder".

Common Credit Pitfalls to Avoid

Now that you have learned some tips on how to improve your credit score and history, we are going to take a look at what *not to do*. This chapter will be entirely focused on common credit pitfalls and ways that you can easily avoid them. While you can make changes to help improve your credit rating and history, much of the changes will come over time from developing healthy financial habits. Here is a list of common credit pitfalls, and ways that you can avoid falling into them:

1.   Making late payments. I think we have made this very clear. Do not make late payments. Not only will the late fee cost you money, but each one will damage your credit. Do what you can to avoid having to pay late fees on your credit accounts. Avoid this by setting up automatic payments or paying your bills as soon as you are paid. There are numerous budget and tracking apps that have reminder features to help you remember. All phones have a calendar feature as well, as do most email accounts. In this age, there is literally no reason to forget paying something on time.

2.   Making the minimum payment only. This can be done for a short while, but after some time you are going to need to pay more than the minimum payment. Otherwise you will continue to struggle to pay down your debt. This is especially the case if you do not have a low interest rate. For credit cards with 20% or higher interest rate that means you are paying thousands of dollars more in interest by the end of your minimum payments. That is money that is going straight to the creditors. Avoid this by including a "debt repayment" amount in your budget category. Anytime you are under budget in another category pay extra towards one debt. Likewise, do not spend more on your credit cards than you can afford to pay in a short period of time.

3.   Maxing out your credit cards. You should consistently be aiming to remain at around 30% utilization for your credit cards. You should never overdraft your credit cards as that comes with an additional fee as well. Do the math to avoid this. Find out how much 30% is of your loan and do not use more than this amount if you can absolutely help it. If you are over this amount, figure out a way to begin bringing down the total.

4.   Not understanding how interest free days work. Working within your credit cards' interest free days can help you avoid paying a

substantial amount in interest. It is important to know how to work with these interest free days so that you can avoid paying extra in interest, but still have the benefit of not having to pay for everything the day you purchase it. Try to push all of your major purchases towards the beginning of the month as this will allow you to have the maximum amount of days available to you to avoid paying interest fees. Each credit card has about 40-55 days before interest charges kick in. But this starts from the beginning of a billing cycle not from each individual purchase. So if you need to make a big purchase, do so at the start of the month when you will have some extra time to pay down the debt with as little interest charges as possible.

5. Frequently using cash advances is a terrible mistake. Cash advances cost you a substantial amount of money in interest and in fees. If you need cash use your debit card, there is usually less fees associated with withdrawing cash from a credit card. If you left your credit card at home and you find you need cash, consider borrowing or using money wise apps like Venmo that allow you to transfer money to friends instantly without paying the cash advance fee. This is especially useful if you are splitting a large meal and need to pay in "cash" or pay right then and there.

6.   Choosing never to use credit cards again. Given all the costs that are associated with credit cards and how many wise choices you need to make, some people turn to cutting credit cards out of their life completely. This is not the best choice to make. I know the temptation, but credit cards can actually be a really useful thing in your life. They help build credit; they help you get rewards that you would not be able to get just by paying cash. To avoid falling into this mistake, be wise about what credit cards you take on. Don't sign up for just any card because they pre-approved you. Instead find the cards that will be most useful to you and your needs. Then invest your time and energy into making those cards work to your benefit instead of swearing off all credit cards forever.

7.   Overspending. This is one of the most common credit card mistakes. It is easy to be tempted to buy something you otherwise would not buy with your cash just because you have the option to pay it off over a longer period of time. But when we continuously do this, we rack up debt that can be incredibly hard to pay off soon. Thus, adding up the amount we will pay in interest. Get a budget and stick to it. If you are going to buy something on a credit card, think about how much you will have to pay per month to pay it off quicker than just by paying the minimum

payment. If you can figure out a plan that won't cost you too much, then go for it. But do the math first before you decide.

8.　　Letting companies share your private information. Often, creditors will send us updated privacy reports with details about what and to who they can sell of our information. Most people toss these without reading them. But take the time to at least skim them. It is important to know where your information might go when you are associated with a creditor. Likewise, many people are unaware, but you can also opt out of info sharing with most companies. They don't make this information clearly available, but if you reach out to customer service you can easily request this. It just takes the time of a phone call and will help keep your information secure.

9.　　Not being aware of associated fees. When you sign up for a new credit account or loan, it can be easy to get caught up in the excitement that you fail to learn everything there is to learn about your credit card. But it important you make yourself fully aware as soon as possible. All credit cards come with associated fees and you need to know what they are so you can avoid them. We all know about late fees, but there are also other types of fees. Often there are fees associated with using the cash advance feature in addition to the higher interest rate you will have to pay. Did you know there are fees for being over the limit? If you max out your cards and then your account is charged with interest, this could mean you are over the limit and will be charged extra for the interest fees. There are fees associated with credit card balance transfers. There are fees associated with returned payments. There are fees for a variety of things and each card has a different policy on when they charge and when they don't. Be sure to know exactly what your card terms are.

10.   Lending out your credit card. Every time you lend your credit card to someone else, you are basically giving them access to your money and an opportunity to ruin your credit score and history. This does not mean that no one can be trusted, it simply means that you need to be cautious about who you trust and with what. Lending your card can be a good way to earn bonus rewards, but aside from that there are many risks with it. Only loan your card out to people you trust who respect your wishes and your financial history.

11.   Closing your accounts after paying them off. This actually has the power to do more harm than good. If you have paid off a debt, do not rush to closing it as a way to rid yourself of the memories of that debt. Instead leave the account open and wait for a time when it will not impact your credit score. If you recall, the longer you have

an account the better this is for your credit score as well. So even if you only use the card to pay for groceries every few months, do not close it unless you absolutely have to. It will be better for your score in the long run.

12.   You apply to more than one or two cards at a time. Remember, recent credit history can impact your credit score and credit report. Applying for many different kinds of credit cards or loans at once will negatively impact your credit. Each application will require a "hard" check on your credit, thus removing a few points from your credit score each time you apply. This is why it is important to only apply to cards that you know you would really like. Only apply for one card at a time. It might be a good idea to organize your desired cards in numerical order, and make sure you actually qualify for the cards you apply for. If you get a rejection, improve your credit and then go to the next one on your list a few months later. Do not just move down the list without actively improving your credit score and credit history.

13.   Avoiding knowing your credit terms. Just like it is important to know what the fees are that are associated with your card, it is also important to know all the terms for your card. Is the lender allowed to change your interest rate at any point? Can they raise your amount available without your permission? What about cancelling

your account or selling your information? This is all information you need to be aware of so that you can make wise choices with your accounts.

14. Do not lose sight of what you want. If you opened the credit card with a specific purpose in mind. Do not lose sight of this. Only use your cards for what you intended to use them on. If your goal was to payoff certain debts with the cards, then only use it for those purposes. If the card was to fund certain travels necessary for work, then only use it for those purposes. The minute you lose sight of your goals is the minute that you begin using your cards on impulsive purchases. Avoid this by only taking your cards with you when you absolutely need to. Do not carry them with you if you are just going to hang out near the mall. It will create temptation that is harder to avoid.

15. You ignore your budget. Do not ignore your budget. If you have a plan for how you are going to payback your debt, it often relies on sticking to your budget in other categories. The minute you start ignoring your budget you end up having to move money from one area to another and things like savings and debt repayment suffer as a result. If you have yet to make a budget, now would be a good time to start. You'll need it if you want to improve your credit score and your credit history.

It's easy to see how people fall into credit card pitfalls like the ones above. People make mistake and very few people understand exactly how credit and credit cards work. By reading this book you are taking active steps towards making sure you keep yourself educated and aware. Be sure to avoid these top fifteen credit card mistakes in order to be successful in building your credit history and raising your credit score.

Funds Creation Blueprint

So you have started a business or are in the process of starting a business and you want to do your best to set it up for success and ensure an influx of cash. How exactly do you do this? Well, a lot of people turn to bootstrapping as a way to bring in income for their businesses from the get-go.

What is bootstrapping?

Bootstrapping basically means that you will be funding your business early by spending as little as possible and turning to your business influx as a way to fund your ongoing expenses. This also means you can start your business without a high amount of startup costs. But bootstrapping is not entirely fool proof, and though it is doable, it requires some forethought and planning. Let's take a look at the pros and cons when it comes to bootstrapping.

Pros and Cons

Pro: You retain full ownership of your company.

When you do not have investors or people who have lent you money, you do not have to worry about their goals colliding with yours. You can make whatever choices you need to make without having to worry about how it will affect other people. This is one of the main reasons that people turn to bootstrapping for their businesses. If freedom is important to you then you may want to find a way to bootstrap your startup costs. Otherwise, if you are willing to work with others and keep their goals and motivations in mind then it might be a good idea to consider looking for an investor or loan.

Con: You can easily find yourself out of business.

Bootstrapping means that you only have a set amount of money to spend. You cannot go and easily request more money if you go out of budget in one category. This is why it is important, that if you choose to bootstrap, you create a clear budget from the beginning. You should also prioritize your costs so that if you have more money you know exactly where that money should be applied as it moves in. If you decide that you do not like the idea of having to budget so early on, then take the time to create a powerful pitch deck and go out and seek investors.

Pro: You are forced to create a plan that will actually work.

When you have no one but yourself to turn to, you begin making much smarter choices. Part of the appeal of bootstrapping for many people is the idea that they must make a plan that will work because they have no one to turn to but themselves. If you have a clear plan for how to spend little as you start up, and how to earn that money back as soon as possible through hard work, then bootstrapping might be for you. It is important you are at least moderately savvy in business topics before you begin however. Taking an online business course, a community college course, or just checking out a plethora of books from the library are just a few ways to educate yourself on business topics prior to beginning your own business.

Con: You have no other help.

It might sound very appealing to be the sole person in charge of your company. But there are a lot of people who struggle to stay afloat when it is only them running the business. Running a business of any kind requires skill in admin work, skill in dealing with customers, planning and budgeting skills, and many other habits beyond this. If you choose to bootstrap you have no one to turn to for advice, or at least not anyone who is as invested in the business as you are. If you feel that you need at least basic mentorship, or someone to handle some other aspect of the business, then bootstrapping might not be the best option for you. It would be wiser to have someone join the company who can potentially help with an area you are unsure about.

Pro: Clear dedication and innovation.

Anytime you are dealing with a business that NEEDS you to bring in income, and that belongs wholly to you, you tend to become more innovative and dedicated. How would your work ethic change if you were working for yourself versus working for someone else? Most of the time people find they waste less time, they are more innovative with solutions, and they prioritize certain tasks. Running your own business with your own money means you will have to be wise about how you use your time and your resources. If you have the drive to do this and trust yourself to make smart choices then bootstrapping might be for you.

Con: Credibility lacks without investors.

Without outside investors, it becomes easy for your company to appear less credible than if you had a set of investors. If you feel you need the credibility to really break into a certain type of business then it might be a good idea to try to bootstrap but also take on an investor. If you do not need any kind of credibility to do well in the type of business you are involved with then, by all means, continue pursuing bootstrapping as an option.

Crowdfunding: What is it?

Crowdfunding is a type of funding that occurs when you collect small amounts of money from a vast amount of people. Crowdfunding is a popular choice for many small business now. There are a variety of type of crowdfunding options that can help you fund your business with little investment on your part.

Types of Crowdfunding

1.   Rewards crowdfunding: This type of crowdfunding typically gives the funding party a type of reward in exchange for their investment. Kickstarter and Indiegogo are two popular resources for this type of funding. Some people offer a discounted rate on their prototype. Other people presell items on these funding sites in exchange for investment up front. This is a good option for people who might be able to offer a product in exchange for getting the funding up front. Sometimes people ask for donated items as a way to offer rewards for their funders.

2.   Donation based: This type of crowdfunding asks people to make small donations as a way to help raise funds for their business. Often, people donate out of a willingness to help the person or a willingness to see the business succeed. There is usually nothing received except for a thank you from the business raising the funds. Some people seek out crowdfunding in this way when they have nothing to offer right away (like those making a film or something similar).

3.   Equity: This type of funding means people buy a small amount of your business as a way for you to gain a small amount of funds. Usually the people buying the business only buy small amounts. It is important, if you choose this type of funding, that you make sure you are maintaining the majority of the business ownership.

4.   Debt crowdfunding: This funding requires lenders who are willing to give a small loan to the company with the expectation that they will make back the principal and then some as part of interest payment. This is a good option for those who expect to make a large profit very soon. There is no reward needed and no equity to be sold. But if you do not know how long it will take to make money, it might be wiser to go towards a different funding source.

Pros and Cons of Crowdfunding

Pro: Low risk

With most reward crowdfunding websites, you do not have to fulfill the reward requirement unless you actually reach your funding amount. That means that there is little risk to begin crowdfunding. You also don't need to pay any fee to sign up. Usually the website takes a small sum from the total raised.

Con: You need to market

If you have absolutely no skills in marketing, it might be difficult to raise money via crowdfunding. You need to be able to get the word out about your business in order to have people donate. Because crowdfunding typically requires a large amount of tiny donations, that means that the more people who donate the better your chances are.

Pro: More exposure

If your business is just getting started, you will likely get more exposure through crowdfunding than you would just by talking about it. In that way, you do spread the word about your business. But remember, you still need some marketing skill to get actual donations.

Con: There are rules

To get funding through crowdfunding you need to follow their rules. The business or product has to fit within a category, and it will be much harder to raise funds if you have a business that is a non-consumer product. Typically, people fund projects that they are interested in using themselves or supporting through another way.

Pro: You get funds before you have an actual product

This will keep your own startup costs very low and help you focus on other important aspects of your business instead of trying to raise funds. Likewise, the people who fund you on crowdfunding sites typically understand that a deliverable will not come for some time. Many do not see a product until years after their initial donations.

Con: Less flexibility

Once you begin a crowdfunding campaign, people are expecting something in return for their donation (most of the time). That means that you do not have as much flexibility with your campaign as you would have if you weren't responding to investors or funders. If you are not sure whether you can get your business up and running in a certain amount of time then it might be best not to seek out most of the crowdfunding options.

Angel Investors: What are they?

An Angel investor is basically someone who is being a symbolic "angel" to your startup. They are there to invest a large amount of money into your startup. They usually invest in exchange for equity, but many angel investors are understanding and do not ask for more than 20% which means you can have two angel investors and still maintain ownership of the majority of your business.

Pros and Cons of Angel Investors:

Pro: Guidance and support is included

Most angel investors want the businesses to succeed because it will yield a higher return on their initial investment. This means they are often willing to help you by offering mentorship or advice. If you want the option of having someone to turn to for advice than this is a good option for you.

Con: Rapid growth is expected

Most angel investors will not sign on to a venture if they do not think that sales and a return on their investment will happen within three to five years. When you work with angel investors, they expect to see a return on their timeline, not necessarily on your timeline.

Pro: Future funding is easier to gain

Once you have one investor you gain some credibility so as you become more successful with your startup you can expect for it to be easier to gain more funding later on should you need it for costs that can help your business keep growing.

Likewise, an angel investor who is seeing a positive return on their investment will likely continue to fund the project as it is needed to help you continue on your path to success.

Con: There is less control.

With investors, you now have new motivations and goals piled on to your own. You will need to listen to their needs as you make choices. You can't stall on some products because it is not exactly what you hoped it would be. Most angel investors are driven by the desire to see a return on their investment while you might be driven by a desire to get everything right. This means that you will need to balance both needs because part of your business belongs to the angel investors.

Pro: Startups are not a problem.

Most angel investors enjoy helping startups because they get a good deal on a business that will succeed, and if they do not expect to see a sale soon, they can pull out before they good too much invested. For this reason, angel investors are good for companies that are just getting started.

Con: It really depends on who you know.

It can be really hard to have access to an angel investor especially if you have no networking communities as a new business owner. If you are making the swap from another industry it could be difficult to find an angel investor. While there may be hundreds of thousands of angel investors willing to invest, only a few thousand startups receive investments from this source.

In conclusion

There are numerous available resources for you as a startup. Even if you go through crowdfunding, there are various types of crowdfunding. As you begin setting up your business plan, you will want to choose a funding that is best for you. If bootstrapping is what most motivates you then follow through with it. Just be sure to weigh the pros and cons of each type of funding so that you make the right choice for your business.

Conclusion

Now that you have finished this book there is a plethora of tools at your disposal. It is time to take what you have learned and begin implementing it for your own benefit. Once easy place to start would be to see where you fit on the credit card ladder and make goals to figure out how to move up the ladder.

If you are focused on improving your credit score, be sure to follow the advice we provided and start making changes for the better. Even if you feel you have a low score, the advice in this book will help you fix those errors and help you make better choices going forward.

For those who are starting a business, hopefully this book has given you some ideas on how you can take what you have learned and fund your business without too much startup costs upfront. Hopefully, you can use one of the business credit options available, along with some bootstrapping, and some funding from outside sources.

This book is not intended to provide everything you need to know, rather it is meant to create a strong foundation of knowledge for those who are looking to expand their understanding of consumer credit. I hope you have found the information and advice useful.

www.ingramcontent.com/pod-product-compliance
Lightning Source LLC
Chambersburg PA
CBHW071645210326
41597CB00017B/2123